the musician's spirit

connecting to others

through story

Other publications by James Jordan available from GIA Publications, Inc.

The Musician's Soul

Meditations for The Musician's Soul
by Fr. Bede Camera, O.S.B., and James Jordan

Evoking Sound: Fundamentals of Choral Conducting and Rehearsing

Evoking Sound: Video
with Heather Buchanan

Choral Ensemble Intonation: Method, Ensemble, and Exercises
Text and video
by James Jordan and Matthew Mehaffey

the MUSICIAN'S *spirit*

connecting to others through story

A companion to the *Musician's Soul*

James Jordan
Westminster Choir College
of Rider University

Foreword by **Eugene Migliaro Corporon**

GIA Publications, Inc.
Chicago

The Musician's Spirit James Jordan
Book art direction and design: Yolanda Durán
Illustrations: Yolanda Durán
Photographs by Michael Kinney. Used with permission.
Photograph on page 176 by Daniel Payn. Used with permission.
Photographs in section "notes, stories and reflections" by Eric Scott Kephart.
Used with permission.

G-5866
ISBN: 1-57999-191-2

7404 S. Mason Avenue, Chicago, IL 60638

www.giamusic.com

Printed in the United States of America.

t o

Florence Mary Jordan

my mother who has enriched and deepened my life.
Through her humanity, care for others, and love
of her family, she has spent her
life giving and loving others.

She has given to me more than I could ever return.

She is the best part of my story.

&

t o

Elizabeth Jarrett Jordan

for her presence and inspiration in my life.
She has caused me to reconsider
and deeply enrich
my own story.

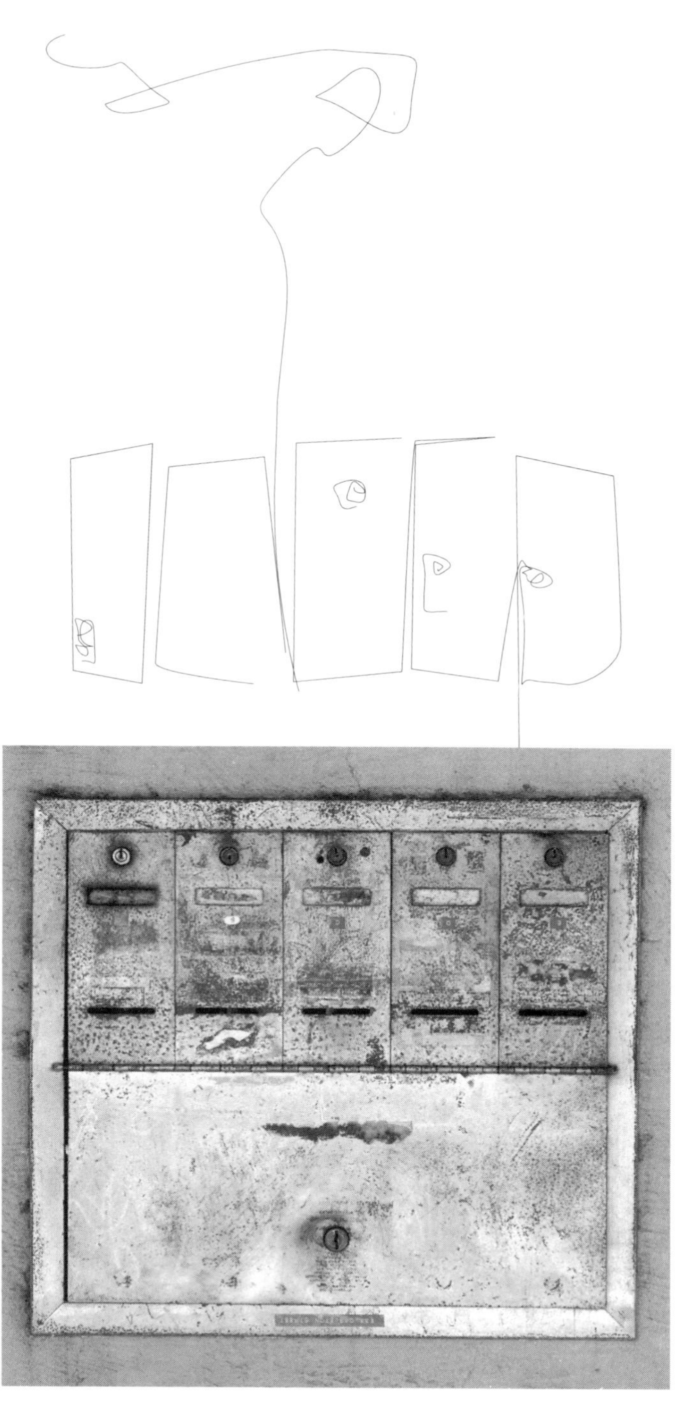

table of contents

Bruce Adolphe

What to Listen
for in the World

You can remember
in your mind
or your body.

When you remember
only in your mind,
your eyes cannot see out,
but only in.
as you visit
images and sounds
your body numb, unmoved;
though you may smile
or sob inside your face.

When you remember
in your body,
you may wail out loud,
bite your lip,
sweat or clench your fist
at a death that happened
twenty years earlier
but is suddenly now.

Every death
and every kiss
can be at any moment now.

When you know
that all is now,
when that death
that kiss
that wound
that glance
that taste
that touch
that breath
are now
in your mind
and in your body
and you can begin
to create
true music
But the opposite
is also true;
listen to true music
and discover
that breath
that touch
that taste
that glance
that wound
that kiss
that death
now in your mind
and in your body.

Used with permission

acknowledgements

Where does one begin? This book was inspired by the stories of so many others. Their stories have intersected with mine in so many remarkable ways. Life has a wonderful way of weaving a rich tapestry of experiences that add depth and color to the human condition. People are the "stuff" of those interactions.

This book is the result of a grand collaboration of many kindred spirits. To Father Mark Kelleher—It was your suggestion of "summer reads" with *Quantum Theology* that started the journey of this book. Your friendship and support are deeply cherished.

The artists who contributed their art, ideas, creativity, and spirit receive my heartfelt thanks. To Daniel Jared Payn—Your beautiful photography will hold an honored place in this volume. Aside from being a young and gifted photographer, you are so important to my story. You will never know the influence your life has played upon mine. While you may be my Godson, you will always be one of my best friends. May this, your first published art, be the first of many more.

To Eric Scott Kephart—You are one of the most creative persons I have ever known. You're an artist, writer, and fashion designer with few equals. You have opened up a new world of art and life to my eyes and soul. Your images and ideas have caused me to look deeply at the world and myself. Your creativity constantly amazes me and has been and will continue to be a deep and abiding inspiration. Your spirit has provided a newfound interiority and depth to my work. Because of you, I am beginning to see the world as a visual artist sees it. May you continue to realize your gifts and continue sharing them with the world.

To Yolanda Duran at GIA—Your artistic vision and creativity take this project far beyond what I could have ever envisioned. I hope that people looking at your art in this book will see it as an intimate connection with the message of this book, as well as cause musicians to understand the beauty in the visual arts. The care and love with which you have treated my work can be seen beautifully in the visual work of art you have created. All artists who look at this book will be touched by your creativity.

To Dominic Gregorio, Susanne Spencer-VanDyke, Lynn Eustis, Nicholas Beck and the St. Gregory's Juggling Troupe, Mattie Stepanek, George Miller, Lenny the Shoeshine Man, Donald Stoppi, George Miller, Florence Jordan, Louis Jordan, Elizabeth Jordan, and Leslie Jordan—Through either your written word or our shared experience, your stories are integral and deepening parts of my life. Thank you for allowing me to publish such personal stories of your lives. I hope that your stories will help everyone who reads this book experience the re-awakening of their own rich narrative life.

To my beloved students at Westminster—May we always remember the stories and the music we shared and will continue to share. May you remember our journeys together, and may you use your stories to teach and make music.

To Alec Harris, Edward Harris, and Robert Batastini—Your faith in my work and the work of so many others can never be repaid. I hope that musicians realize the gift you have given to our profession through your courage to publish. For the past thirty years, GIA has supported and given a voice to those of us who may have never had an opportunity to be heard. For that, I will always be deeply grateful. And to my editor, Denise Wheatley from GIA—for contributing your meticulous editiorial skills to this project. You polished my manuscript—thanks!

Finally, a few last words on this book. A quote by Thomas Moore in *The Soul's Religion* has occupied much of my thinking in these days. Spiritual emptiness as defined by him is approaching life with both an open mind and an open self.

If any religious or spiritual act is lacking sacred emptiness, it becomes full of itself and turns into its opposite, a defensive edifice against the cleansing power of mystery. Spiritual teachings are of two kinds: those that are heavy and opaque, consisting in spiritual facts and required teachings, and those that are light and transparent, always pointing beyond themselves and never fully graspable. It's a rare pleasure to find a teacher or a teaching comfortable with this lightness and willing to be glass rather than stone **(p.11).**

This book may be simple, but it is not naïve. The concept of story is simple, yet powerful and compelling. I have tried to walk the fine line between over-teaching and staying out of the way so that the reader can be in charge of his own journey through story. The best teachers I have had in my life are those that intimately understood that teaching is about not teaching. To make too much of a teacher is to miss the chance to learn. The best teachers, I feel, work within a narrow boundary of profound irony where they assume the role of a fool. It is their job to assist in discovery and awaken the memory.

I hope that in some small way, I, with the help of all the persons above, have succeeded.

Man is a messenger who forgot the message. **(p. 43)**

Abraham Joshua Heschel

I Asked for Wonder

The more uncertain I have felt about myself,
The more there has grown up in me a feeling
Of kinship with all things.

C.G. Jung

Memories, Dreams, Reflections

—James Jordan

Princeton

foreword by James Jordan

It has been almost five years since I began writing *The Musician's Soul.* Just as that book allowed me to think about various issues through the written word, this book has as well. I've learned that in order for musicians to become great performers or great teachers, they must know themselves intimately. I've also learned that it is the responsibility of the artists to see how the world at large is reflected in and through their art.

So many of us spend so much time at our craft that we sometimes miss the soul stories in our music. As I will discuss later, *The Musician's Soul* dealt with helping people take inward journeys and allowing them to know themselves better. But after one has been "inside," how does one reconnect to the world at large, and more specifically, to those with whom we make music?

In searching for a title for this book, the word "spirit" kept returning to my mind. If "soul" is the inner manifestation of one's spirituality and inward life, then what do we call what others perceive? Spirit seems to fit. One perceives the spirit of a person. One reacts to the spirit of a teacher or a musician. So, it is spirit that one projects to people through their music. That spirit is an external embodiment of one's inward life.

Spirit has an interesting dictionary definition: Spirit 1) A vital force that characterizes a living being as being alive. 2) Somebody's will or sense of self, or enthusiasm for living. 3) Somebody or something that is divine, inspiring, or animating influence.

Are these definitions not what a musician feels or experiences on a regular basis? To take the definition one step further, are these not the qualities that are perceived by

James Jordan

others when a musician is engaged in their art? Are we aware that while we believe people are responding to our knowledge of the music, what they are actually responding to is the spirit that is transmitted to the ensemble or other musicians involved in the music-making process?

So, the journey of this book is set. Through it, you will learn how to share yourself and your artistic being with others after you have made your own personal inner journey. You will discover how stories play a role in the life of a musician. You will realize that great teachers and musicians become great because they partake in meaningful sharing. To be able to give of oneself is the greatest gift a teacher and artist can give.

In light of 9-11-01, let us rededicate ourselves to sharing even more through our music so that music and the arts become a major force against hatred and inhumanity. During these past months, I have been thankful that I am a musician, because the music that I experience as a performer helps me make sense of this world. May you all be helped to share yourselves and your spirits in a more meaningful way through the ideas, images, and stories in this book.

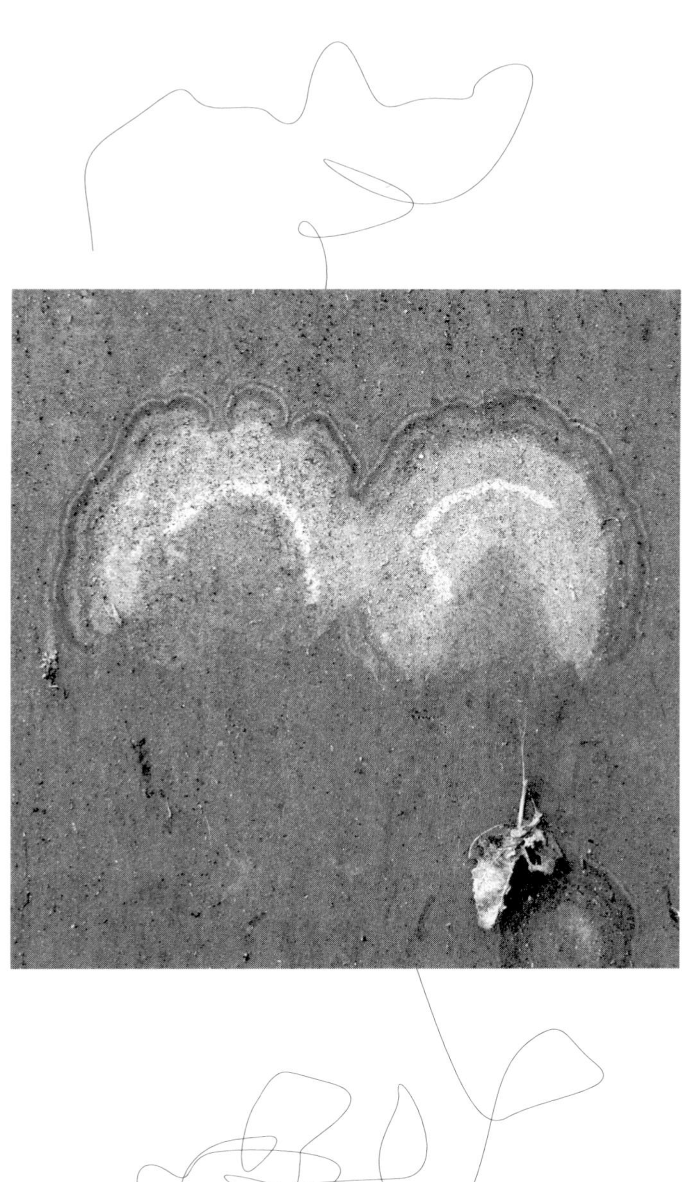

foreword by Eugene Migliaro Corporon "The Boomerang Book"

This book is about storying and I have one to share. I first became aware of James Jordan when I read *The Musicians Soul.* Like most people who have read his work, the thoughts and feelings that I was led to overwhelmed me. I am not a person who reads a volume of this magnitude without being fully armed. In order to participate in the act of reading I must be equipped with a myriad of colored pencils and pens. If I anticipate that the book is a real find, and this book was, I will mark it with a rubber stamp that I had made up thirty years ago that says: "Stolen from Eugene Corporon." Because James' books encourage interaction and create a flow of seemingly endless responses, I found myself marking, underlining, highlighting, interpreting; doing my utmost to fill every inch of blank space with my reactions. In the end, this created a sort of personal journal. My copy of *The Musicians Soul* soon became a treasured diary documenting my own spiritual journey.

I share this information with you so that you can understand what a devastating event it was when I left my cherished book in the back of the seat in front of me on a May flight to the East coast. The moment I realized my horrific blunder I called the American Airlines lost and found department. Alas, my precious book had vanished and was nowhere to be found.

Fast-forward several months to September. Early in the fall concert season, I was approached by one of my flute players at a rehearsal. She said she had a surprise for me. Reaching into her music bag, like a magician pulling a rabbit out of a hat, she retrieved my copy of **the lost book.** I was dumbfounded. "Where did you get this? How could you have this? This just isn't possible!" She told me that her Aunt was on a recent flight to New York and had discovered the book in the seat pocket in front of her, apparently right where I had left it five months earlier. She went on to tell me that her Aunt remembered a conversation they had had about how much she enjoyed being in the Wind Symphony at the University of North Texas. She thought she remembered the name stamped in the front of the book from that discussion. Seeing the vast array of hieroglyphics and notes in the margins, she realized its importance to me and decided to see that it was returned. This experience made it clear to me that I was meant to have this book. This particular book. I also realized that its re-entry into my life was a sign that I had many more lessons to learn from its contents. As you might expect, James Jordan's work has even greater spiritual significance to me because of this concurrence.

The Musicians Spirit should come with Velcro strips so that you can permanently attach it to your body. The work is an essential and inspirational resource that guides one to resonating music's messages. It is full of "fantasy and wonder" and can be thought of as a kind of secret decoder that demystifies what was thought to be an unbreakable code. It is a book that will not take long to read. It is also a book that you will never finish. Storying and Musicing are one in the same. One uses words, the other uses sound. Both have a profound impact on the way we perceive the world. These are musical stories from the heart, which can guide us to life-lessons with deep meaning. James reminds us that the soul grounds us and the spirit frees us to soar. This book will cause you to "explore and discover," and encourages you to allow your spirit to express your soul. It celebrates curiosity, creativity, and compassion. This publication provides a way to link our lives to the people we love through the music we make. While mastery is important, mystery is music's true purpose. Great music and great musicing has always had a sense of mystery about it. James challenges us to become mystics and investigate our past in order to guide our future. Connecting with others is the ultimate reason for being and doing. By guiding the journey inward to and through our own lives, James Jordan puts each of us closer to and more in touch with that purpose.

Eugene Migliaro Corporon
Director of Wind Studies
University of North Texas, Texas

note from the art director

I have often found myself describing visual compositions using musical terms, such as "The colors in that painting are in perfect *harmony*" or "His collages have a *jazzy* feel to them." At the same time, music can and is described as having texture, color, flavor, density, etc. In the arts, vocabulary is quite often borrowed from one medium to describe another with great ease, perhaps because most artists are striving to provoke an emotional response from their audience.

George Gershwin's *Rhapsody in Blue* is an excellent example of how vocabulary so often used to describe the visual arts works perfectly to describe a musical number. When I first heard this musical piece, I thought, What a great title. I can't imagine any other color describing the sound/music created by Gershwin. Blue is the color I see when I am listening to it. It brings about a feeling of peace and tranquility, but at the same time energy and freedom. When the conceptual team behind the United Airlines' television spots decided to use *Rhapsody in Blue* in their commercials, I am sure they were well aware of the emotional response they could draw from consumers. Perhaps this is why they filmed a United Airlines airplane traveling over an immense and infinite blue sky, forever engraving into our subconscience a feeling of peace and safety.

So when I was asked to work on James Jordan's *The Musician's Spirit*—a book for musicians, I was very excited. After I read the manuscript and had several conversations with James, I felt that the content would enrich any artist's experience—the artists did not necessarily have to be musicians. Moved by the content, I had to now describe it visually. At first, I suffered through a mental block. Then I forced myself to visit the basics, including the visual language that musicians use to record their compositions. Though I myself cannot read music, I have long admired the beauty of this language: the pattern formed by the staves, and the visual movement created by the notes as they progress across the page.

While researching another project, I came across the compositions of Sylvano Bussotti, an Italian composer. I remembered being fascinated by his visual compositions. The elegance of the undulating line, the sharp exacting movement of the line, and the geometric shapes included in these compositions I found irresistible. All of this beauty was created by a simple black line over a white background. This same black line, which turns, curves, becomes thick then thin, and forms angles, also creates type. The simple black line would be the focus for the design of *The Musician's Spirit.*

I have attempted to capture the simple beauty of the black line throughout the book. I have "borrowed" from Bussotti's compositions and have created my own. In some of my illustrations, I have attempted to mimick the musical notes; in others, I have focused exclusively on movement. The same concept of the black line was applied to Michael Kinney's photographs. I wanted to transform his images. I wanted the audience to view Kinney's images as objects rather than lanscape or a cropped image. By this means, I believed, the audience would remain focused on the black texture and line over the white background—again focusing on the simplicity of the black line.

I hope that the reader will derive some pleasure from the visuals created for *The Musician's Spirit.* I know I took great pleasure in creating them.

Yolanda Durán
Chicago

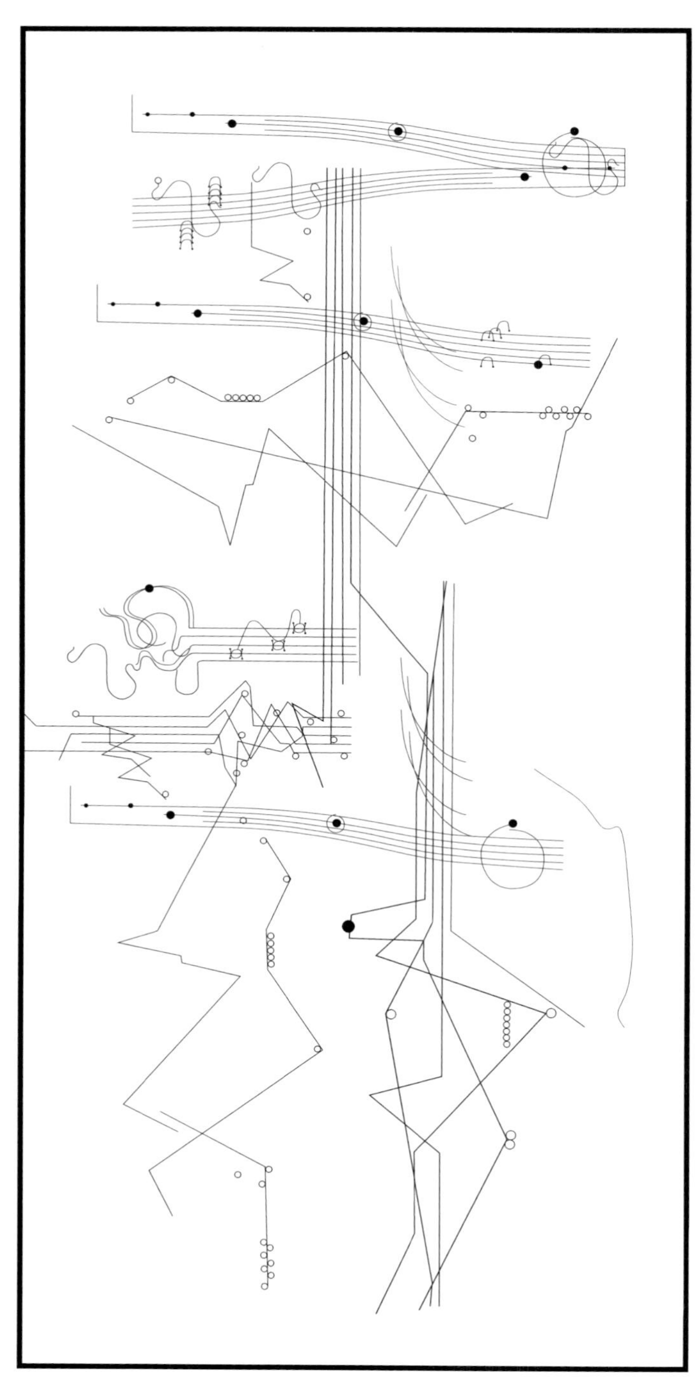

prologue quotations

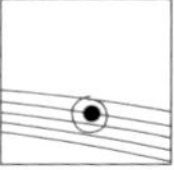

The need to be normal is the predominant anxiety disorder in modern life. **(p. 116)**

Thomas Moore

The Original Self

We who lived in concentration camps can remember the men who walked through the huts comforting others, giving away their last piece of bread. They may have been few in number, but they offer sufficient proof that everything can be taken from a man but one thing: the last of human freedoms—to choose one's attitude in any given set of circumstances, to choose one's own way.

Victor Frankl

Man's Search for Meaning

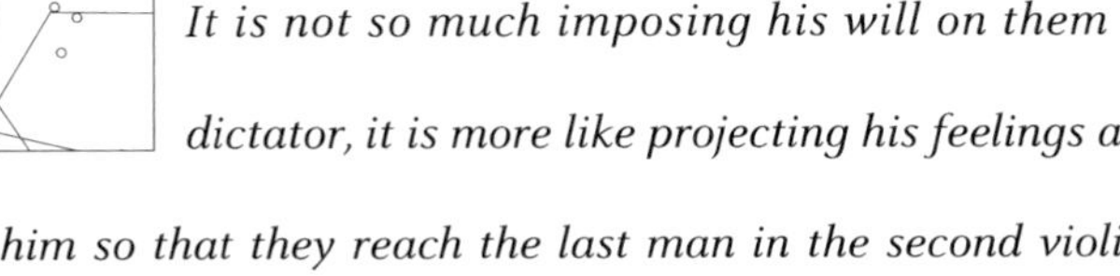

It is not so much imposing his will on them like a dictator, it is more like projecting his feelings around him so that they reach the last man in the second violin section. And when this happens—when one hundred men share

his feelings, exactly, simultaneously, responding as one to each rise and fall of music...then there is human identity of feeling that has no equal elsewhere. **(p. 150)**

Leonard Bernstein

The Joy of Music

If I don't challenge myself to grow inside every single day, I'm limiting my ability to be a more effective person on the podium. I keep a diary every day and its about my inner person; how has it changed today or how it has been challenged today—how has the challenge been met. And if a student says something in rehearsal that upsets me that I think was out of line, through writing about the experience I may realize that, 'Hey that my pride was hurt, I better deal with this myself. There's no need to cause a retribution scene here.' Of course, along with inner growth is cognitive growth. I think when I want to be in the affective but the more cognitive things I can discover to translate the affective, It's just worth it to keep teaching, it's exciting to do it. It's unlimited. **(p. 88)**

Weston Noble

Conducting With Feeling by ***Frederick Harris***

The spiritual landscape, rather than the religious tradition, has become the arena for theological exploration. And the theological excursion may no longer begin with God and work downward; rather, it will originate in the human experience of searching and seeking and move outward to embrace even wider horizons of life and reality. (p. 21)

Diarmuid O'Murchu

Quantum Theology

Believe nothing, no matter where you read it or who has said it, not even if I have said it, unless it agrees with your own reason and your own common sense

Buddha

To transform the world, we must begin with ourselves. However small the world we live in, if we can transform ourselves, bring about a radically different point of view in our daily existence, then perhaps we shall effect the world at large, the extended relationship with others. (p. 2)

J. Krishnamurti

Intimacy and Solitude

I

introductory prologue

the story

vehicle
for
the
musical
journey

Much of what passes for education effects not the re-storying of the soul, of course, but the de-storying. Indeed, the failures of our educational system have been much decried. When perceived and carried out as the transmission of a given body of knowledge into our passively waiting brains, whether we want it or not, it can curtail our curiosity, kill our creativity, and leave us immune to the love of learning.
(p. 242)

To suggest we are stories, to merely have or tell stories, may unsettle us with the suggestion that the ground on which we stand is merely shifting sand; that, even at our healthiest, our 'identity' is not a single reality but a multiple one; that, at best, we are a tangle of tales and, at worst a pack of lies. In addition, while alluding to the creative role we play in the process of our own becoming, such a title can imply that built into who we are is far more an element of our detachment from our own existence than we might otherwise wish to acknowledge; and that, although some detachment is inevitable by virtue of self-consciousness by itself, we are less active livers of our lives than we are passive readers, watchers, or even dreamers of them. **(p. 11)**

William Lowell Randall

The Stories We Are

Stories are designed to force us to consider possibilities. Stories hint that our taken-for-granted daily realities may, in fact, be fraught with surprise. **(p. 110)**

William J. Bausch

Quantum Theology

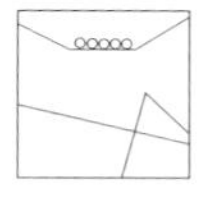

The point I wish to highlight here is that story is the most dynamic and versatile tool available to us humans for the exploration of meaning and mystery. **(p. 110)**

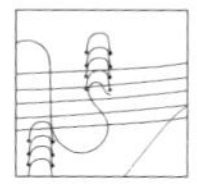

Not only is story at the heart of scientific pursuit, but science itself, in common with all other forms of

wisdom, is born out of story. It is very much the product of humankind's need to make sense and meaning out of life. **(p. 113)**

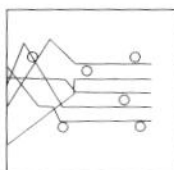

Ultimate meaning is embedded in story, not in facts. **(p. 117)**

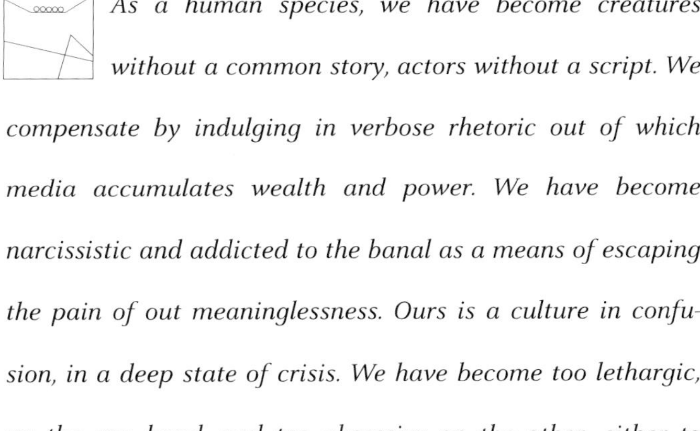

As a human species, we have become creatures without a common story, actors without a script. We compensate by indulging in verbose rhetoric out of which media accumulates wealth and power. We have become narcissistic and addicted to the banal as a means of escaping the pain of out meaninglessness. Ours is a culture in confusion, in a deep state of crisis. We have become too lethargic, on the one hand, and too obsessive on the other, either to listen to or narrate our story. **(p. 119)**

It is at the level of imagination that contemporary life is weakest. With two-thirds of humanity struggling to meet basic survival needs and the other third largely preoccupied with accumulating and hoarding wealth, the human capacity for reflection, intuition, and thought, buttressed by our utilitarian, stereotyped educational system, has all but usurped the artist within us. Ours is a body without a soul, dispirited by uninspired architects, bent on conquering and controlling the objective world.

Some are striving to tell the story anew. It is an uphill struggle against the forces of apathy, ignorance and cynicism. The apathetic won't even listen; perhaps they don't know how to listen among the din and confusion of our time. The ignorant choose not to listen.

The storyteller is unassailable, and when we "rediscover fire" in the many new stirrings of our time, then the storyteller will emerge again 'to save those who have no imagination.'—George Bernard Shaw **(p. 120)**

Diarmuid O'Murchu

Quantum Theology

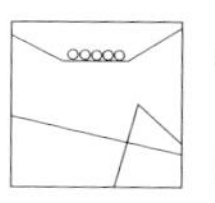

In a long passage on memory in his Confessions, Saint Augustine says that we understand everything in relation to what we have remembered. Memory not only gives us personal remembrances of events, but also archetypal images, a memory not only of things that were but also of things that always are. By calling to mind the various ways in which human life can be lived, we broaden and deepen our imagination, and life opens up to us.

Memory requires certain arts that cultivate it and tease out its many variations and possibilities. Telling stories from childhood or simply from the past brings memory into play. A certain kind of meditation might activate memory, and what may seem to be distractions during meditation—the insistence of memories—may be just what is needed. The memories that pop up spontaneously during a moment of absorption nurture the imagination and educate the emotions.

Memory holds us together as individuals and as communities. When we forget who we have been, we lose a full sense of who we are. People who have drifted apart from the soul or who want to defend themselves against the pain of experience often make an effort to erase memories. They move away from the actual scene of pain, tear down buildings associated with tragedy, or at a personal level, they get as busy as possible so that memory will not have chance to penetrate their consciousness. Memory is potent. It does something to us. It makes us who we are. It gives us depth. It ties our past to our present to overcome the disjunction of a too literal life. It focuses our attention on the imagination of events rather than on events taken literally. Memory is a kind of poetry. **(p. 21–22)**

Thomas Moore

Original Self

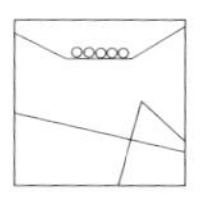

The beyond is not what is infinitely remote, but what is nearest at hand. (p. 376)

Dietrich Bonhoffer

Letters and Papers from Prison

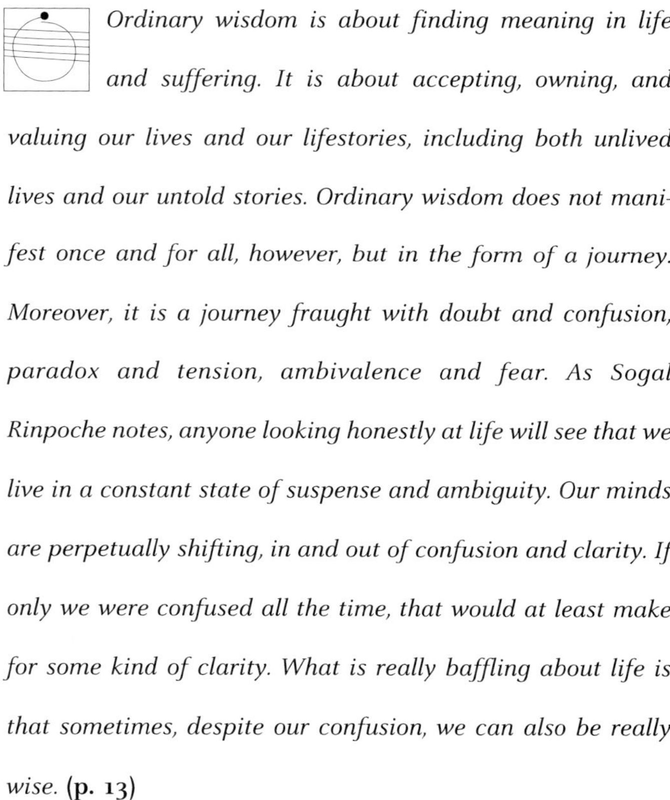

Ordinary wisdom is about finding meaning in life and suffering. It is about accepting, owning, and valuing our lives and our lifestories, including both unlived lives and our untold stories. Ordinary wisdom does not manifest once and for all, however, but in the form of a journey. Moreover, it is a journey fraught with doubt and confusion, paradox and tension, ambivalence and fear. As Sogal Rinpoche notes, anyone looking honestly at life will see that we live in a constant state of suspense and ambiguity. Our minds are perpetually shifting, in and out of confusion and clarity. If only we were confused all the time, that would at least make for some kind of clarity. What is really baffling about life is that sometimes, despite our confusion, we can also be really wise. (p. 13)

William L. Randall

Ordinary Wisdom

In *The Musician's Soul* (GIA, 1999), much of what I wrote asked you to take an inward personal journey. That book asked you to examine many aspects of your "interior self" so that it could become a major catalyst in your music making. The assumption of the book was that if you understand vulnerability and center, and take time to understand yourself, then honesty, directness, and simplicity would be transferred through you to the music and vice versa.

The major premise of *The Musician's Soul* is the principle of mimetics. Hopefully the mimetical tools in that book would allow you to stay "in a good place" longer, perhaps for the entire duration of a musical rehearsal, class, lesson, or concert. That book asked you to connect with yourself.

The Musician's Spirit has another important objective that builds upon the ideas in *The Musician's Soul.* This book attempts to help with the complicated problem of connecting with others and with the music. While being able to love oneself, accept oneself, and really get to know oneself is a powerful tool, this book attempts to present the case of one of the musician's most powerful tools, which is *the story.*

If you pause to think about the great teachers in your life, whether they are conductors of music or teachers in another subject area, you will find that they are all skillful artists of the story. They understand stories and words that may not be about *things,* but can still relate to their lives. Those of us who have sung with the late Robert Shaw saw that he was a great storyteller. He told stories that were not about him, but about his relationship with the music. They were stories about the musical journeys that he'd already taken before the rehearsal ever began. He let you in on his inward journey. Great musicians and teachers like Shaw use words to show how the art they attempt to create has profound meaning in their lives.

The book from which I draw quotes at the start of this chapter, *Quantum Theology,* has had a major influence on my thinking and has given me a valuable wake-up call. This book goes through lengthy explanations that address why quantum physics and theology will merge during this century. This is a fascinating concept. However, toward the end of the book, a very poignant question is posed: How will this union take place? The answer is through *story!* These stories will be personal and keep one connected to the human experience in a very complex, ever changing world. When I encountered that concept, I realized that the story is one of the most important rehearsal techniques.

I remember once talking to a Catholic priest about this story "thing" and relating my bubbling enthusiasm for my new revelation. He calmly replied, "Oh, yes." Then he told me that the sermons involving his own personal life experiences have the most profound and far-reaching affect on his parishioners.

When speaking of one's stories or life experiences, one seems to enter a sacred area where listening becomes more profound, and the spoken word is given a more direct track into the listeners own soulfulness. Where does one look for the repository of such stories? If one has taken the suggested journeys in *The Musician's Soul,* then the beginnings of stories are in place. The library of such stories is our lives.

The Musician's Spirit is a bit different from *The Musician's Soul.* In *The Musician's Soul,* each chapter attempts to take you on a carefully self-guided tour of your inner workings. The book asks you to gain a new appreciation of love and care for yourself and the people with whom you make music. *The Musician's Spirit* is designed for artists and music-makers, i.e. classroom teachers, conductors, studio teachers, and composers; all those who are involved in music making on all levels. It is a book that you can keep with you

Musician's Spirit

and open before a rehearsal if you need help getting "in the right place."

This book has three vehicles. The first vehicle is the short essay, the second vehicle is short quotes, and the third vehicle is visual art.

The first vehicle, the short essay, attempts to give you "sample stories." These are *my* life stories. There are also stories from others. I am continually amazed by the number of meaningful stories that occur in our lives daily. But because we sometimes live our lives unaware, we miss these life lessons. Great musicians, on the other hand, are great observers of the human condition and are aware (sometimes painfully aware) of life throbbing around them. Their stories allow them to find profound meaning in the music they teach or conduct.

It is also remarkable to me that each of us has a wealth of stories in our memory from the early part of our lives; back when real joy and innocence didn't get buried underneath the weight of life's complexity. Our new mission should be to scrape away those life barnacles so that we can retell the stories of early life and experience that joy again. This way, we can cry in a different way, remember what it is to play again so that we can play with our music, and truly live life from the inside out.

I always marveled at the greatest influence in my musical life, Dr. Elaine Brown. A wonderful musician, yes. Her rehearsals were not loaded with complex, technical details. Yet, her Singing City choirs always sang as Dr. Brown so often said, "Better than they really could." How did she do it? By being a great teller of stories, that's how. She told life stories—real life stories—that were honest. Stories that when told, at times, jolted me into a connection with myself (and many times others) that I had either not experienced for a long time or had never experienced. She, through her life and the stories she told, caused my soul to soar and explore. And when I soared and explored, so did the music.

Lesson learned and noted, Dr. Brown.

My stories are about some things in my life that I think will trigger stories that you have. I am sure that when you read the story titled *The Rocket Ship,* you will laugh with me and remember something you did that allowed you as a child to take a fantasy journey. I have also included stories of others that they generously contributed to this volume. These stories involve a teacher who did not love a student, a music teacher who suffered a stroke and now looks at each day differently, and a group of high school men who juggled their way through Europe with no money. These stories caused me to take journeys that I needed to take, and I hope they do the same for you. As we live through the horrors of the World Trade Center bombing, it is the stories that make us weep. It is those stories that touch our souls and make us feel human through an event that dehumanized us all. In reality, everyone who we lost had his or her stories, too.

The second vehicle is quotes. About a year ago, a woman gave me the inspiration for this book when she asked, "What do I do when, in the course of day, I find myself in need of a spiritual 'lift,' or 'redirection?' Is there anything I can give my choir or band to read quickly before a rehearsal that will 'put them in the right place?' It takes too much time to hunt for the 'right' quote in your books."

This woman's question inspired me to arrange the quotes and stories in this book according to headings so that different points can be found easily. The quotes are also indexed according to topic for easy reference. On those pages where there are quotes, there is often artwork. I wanted this book to be artistically beautiful, and the artists I chose to work on it have a gift for artistic clarity.

I want people to have this book in their briefcases, in their choir folders, or on their office desks. I want it to function as a portable art gallery. I want it to be a source of inspiration and redirection so that the essence of teaching can be at everyone's fingertips.

When I wrote *The Musician's Soul,* I asked a highly respected musician to write the foreword. The response was, "That's impossible to write about." A number of years later, the same person said that I talk too much in rehearsals. Both points are probably true. However, I am foolish enough to believe that as artists, we have been denied this type of material...material that will keep us focused, motivated, and inspired. And for those of us who struggle day-to-day to bring music to people in both less than agreeable situations and the most desirable situations, there is a need for someone to start somewhere. Dr. Brown always used to tell her students not to be afraid to "be a fool." Because of this, I guess I am not afraid to be a "fool" in hopes that my foolishness will make music making one of the joys of our lives. I also hope that it will help us see the world and the people that inhabit our lives in a newer, more brilliant light.

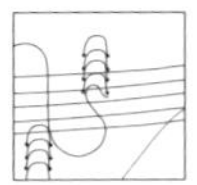

Let us begin by saying that, though some stories seem innocuous, no story is ever innocent. Even the humblest bedtime tale seeks to drive home a point to an impressionable audience. (**p. 69**)

Life is inseparable from story. We live in story and story lives in us. Though simple to state, it can be complex to comprehend and can quickly slip our grasp. Once we grasp it and take seriously the idea of the stories we are, however, we open a Pandora's box of conceptual implications that are not soon pondered. One implication we want to ponder now is that, just as the shape of a life is a story shape and the content of a life is story content, so the meaning of a life is story meaning. **(p. 69)**

Central to the transformation of life into lifestory and raw events into experiencable episodes, we would propose, is narrative intelligence, a capacity on which psychology has been remarkably mute. Although we have been telling stories for eons, the actual skills involved in doing so have received comparatively little attention. **(p. 41)**

William L. Randall

Ordinary Wisdom

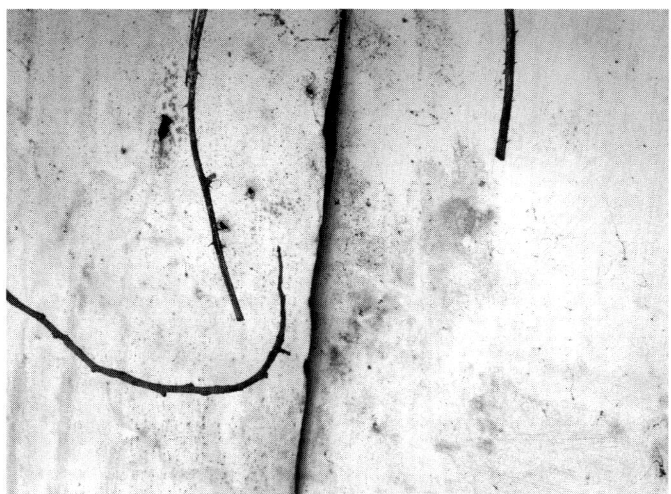

It is all a question of story. We are in trouble just now because we are in between stories. **(p. 110)**

Thomas Berry

Quantum Theology

required reading for artists

In the past several years, I have been asked by many what books should be required reading outside of music for artists. So I have taken on the charge and compiled a list of books from the twentieth century that I believe are "must reads." I do not list specific editions or publishers because many of the books exist in many forms.

Black Elk	*Black Elk Speaks*
Dietrich Bonhoffer	*Letters and Papers from Prison*
Martin Buber	*I and Thou*
Gilbert Keith Chesterdon	*Orthodoxy*
Fyodor Dostoevsky	*The Brothers Karamazov*
T.S. Elliot	*Four Quartets*
Abraham Joshua Heschel	*God in Search of Man* *The Sabbath*
Thich Naht Hahn	*Interbeing*
John XXIII	*Journal of a Soul*
Shunryu Suzuki	*Zen Mind, Beginner's Mind*
Teilhard de Chardin	*The Phenomenon of Man*
St. Therese of Liseux	*The Story of a Soul*
Simone Weil	*Waiting for God*
Elie Weisel	*Night*
William Butler Yeats	*Collected Poems*

James Jordan

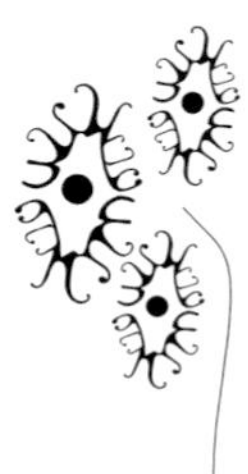

To laugh often and much, to win the respect of intelligent people and the affection of children, to earn the appreciation of honest critics and endure the betrayal of false friends, to appreciate beauty, to find the best in others, to leave the world a bit better, whether by a healthy child, a garden patch...to know even one life has breathed easier because you have lived. This is to know you have succeeded.

Ralph Waldo Emerson

Sometimes our spiritual programmes take us far away from our inner belonging. We become addicted to the programmes of psychology and religion. We become so desperate to learn to be that our lives pass, and we neglect the practice of being. One of the lovely things in the Celtic mind was its sense of spontaneity. Spontaneity is one of the greatest spiritual gifts. To be spontaneous is to escape the cage of the ego by trusting that which is beyond self. One of the greatest enemies of spiritual belonging is the ego. The ego does not reflect the real shape of one's individuality. The ego is the false self born out of fear and defensiveness. The ego is a protective crust that we draw around our affections. It is created out of timidity, the failure to trust the Other and to respect our own otherness. The ego is threatened, competitive, and stressed, whereas the soul is drawn more towards surprise, spontaneity, the new and the fresh. **(p. 118)**

John O'Donahue

Anam Cara

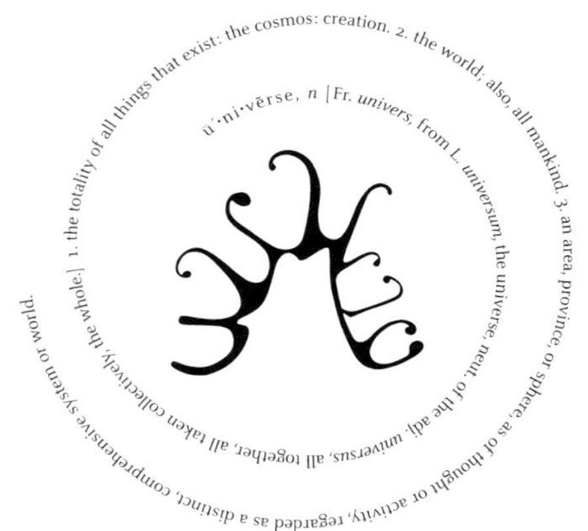
ū´·ni·vērse, n [Fr. univers, from L. universum, the universe, neut. of the adj. universus, all together, all taken collectively, the whole.] 1. the totality of all things that exist: the cosmos: creation. 2. the world; also, all mankind. 3. an area, province, or sphere, as of thought or activity, regarded as a distinct, comprehensive system or world.

Kilgore Trout once wrote a short story, which was a dialogue between two pieces of yeast. They were discussing the possible purposes of life as they ate sugar and suffocated in their own excrement. Because of their limited intelligence, they never came close to guessing that they were really making champagne.

Kurt Vonnegut, Jr.

Breakfast of Champions

II
farming and the musician

Be patient, therefore, brethren, until the coming of the Lord.

James 5:7

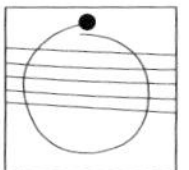

My father was a farmer, and he raised that most rare and exotic crop peculiar to New England, cranberries, a tough and exotic piece of fruit not given to easy entreaty or easy growth....

One day when we were in the garden and I was a young fellow, I told my father that I thought I wanted to go into the ministry. He looked at me, and he said, without changing any one of his attitudes toward his hoeing, "I always hoped that my son would do honest work." I knew what he meant. The farmer lives in proximity to two ultimate truths, which are held in balance by the authority of his own experience. Ultimate truth number one is that the harvest is the result of incredible patience, and ultimate truth number two is that the harvest is the result of incredible work. Yes, he waits and hopes for the autumn and the spring rains, and there is nothing that he can do to induce them. That is where patience comes in. That is where relying on forces beyond one's control comes in. In that season of waiting, however, he is hardly idle, for the farmer does all the work that can and must be done, knowing that time and God alone will bring fruition to what he expects and assists. I have never known an idle farmer who is a good farmer. It is constant work, but the work is full of expectation and fueled by the labor of experience. The farmer knows that what is expected is worth waiting for. The farmer also knows that what is worth waiting for is also worth working for, and that is why the farmer is commended by James in this most practical of epistles. James is not writing to farmers, he is writing to a fairly sophisticated audience of people like ourselves, in having lost the use of their hands in the fields, are now held hostage to the fantasies and disappointments of their minds. (p. 7)

Peter Gomes

SERMONS: Biblical Wisdom for Daily Living

shoetrician

Remember that there is meaning beyond absurdity. Know that every deed counts, that every word is power. Above all, remember that you must build your life as if it were a work of art. **(p. ix)**

The beginning of faith is not a feeling for the mystery of living or a sense of awe, wonder and amazement. The root of religion is the question what to do with feeling for the mystery of living, what to do with awe, wonder and amazement.

Religion begins with a consciousness that something is asked of us.

It is in that tense, eternal asking in which the soul is caught and which man's power is elicited. (p. 38)

Awe is an intuition for the dignity of all things, a realization that things are not only are what they are but also stand, however remotely, for something supreme.

Awe is a sense for the transcendence, for the reference everywhere to mystery beyond all things. It enables us to perceive in the world intimations of the divine...to sense the ultimate in the common and the simple; to feel in the rush of the passing the stillness of the eternal. What we cannot comprehend by analysis, we become aware of in awe. **(p. 3)**

Abraham Joshua Heschel

I Asked for Wonder

Musician's Spirit

Shoetrician Shoe Repair—We're not God, but we do save soles!

The sign in the window caught my eye as I walked past 255 West 40th Street in New York City. It read, "Shoetrician Shoe Repair—We're not God, but we do save soles!" I looked down at my shoes and decided that they needed a shine, so I walked in.

I was immediately greeted by a bundle of life named Lenny. Lenny asked, "Need a shine?" I replied, "Absolutely," and started toward the chair. Lenny spoke up, "Hold on there. You need to know what I do and how much it will cost you. This is not like any other shine you have ever received."

The statement took me aback. *A shine is a shine,* I thought.

"You know, I spit shine." Lenny's eyes had engaged mine.

He's serious about this, I thought.

"Have you ever had a spit shine?" he asked.

"Yes" I replied, "I think one time in San Antonio."

"You haven't had one like mine," he said.

"What's the difference?" I asked. "A shine is a shine."

"I am in every shine I do. I have shined shoes for 35 years in the same place, every working day of my life. I *love* shining shoes. And this will cost you a bit more than the regular shine, and it will take longer. I don't do short shines. You have the time?" asked Lenny.

I was hooked and very curious at this point. "Sure, I have the time. Go to it," I said.

Lenny motioned me up on the chair and he began preparations, which could only be classified as a ritual. He got all his rags, about seven of them, all laid out. He opened several containers and laid them neatly in a row at my feet. He then stepped toward me, touched my shoes, and stood silently for a minute or so with his eyes closed. Then he opened his eyes.

"Shoes have souls you know," he said. "I always try to feel the spirit that is in the shoes. I don't think I shine shoes. I just bring to the surface what is inside."

As Lenny prepared to shine my shoes, there was no talking. This was obviously a careful process. As he began, he said, " So, you are a musician?"

In amazement, I answered, "Yes. How did you know that?"

Lenny said, "It's in the shoes."

I couldn't believe this. A man shining my shoes was turning a simple shoeshine into a soulful experience. And I must say, as he worked on my shoes, a relaxing calm came over me.

Lenny started to apply wax. After that, he began to wrap his hands in rags in a very precise manner. Then he stepped up to my shoes and began to dance! Within the rhythm of that dance, he began to buff. Step, step, buff, buff. Step, step, buff, buff. The snap of the buffing rag added complexity to the danced rhythm. It was almost like Lenny was transported to another place to shine my shoes. And it was clear to me (and my shoes) that buffing my shoes was the most important thing in the world at this moment to Lenny.

"You see, I also put energy back into shoes. Shoes have people's souls in them. Believe me, I have experienced a lot of souls in this shop over the years. I am very rich because I have experienced so many people through their shoes. I love this job...it is the best job in the world."

Lenny danced, buffed, and polished for 45 minutes. When he was done, my shoes had become a work of art! He stepped back with a look of incredible pride. "See, I told you. My shines are special. This shine will last for weeks."

And you know what? The shine lasted for months, and I swear his touch changed those shoes. They are still my most comfortable and favorite shoes.

I have thought a lot about Lenny and the parallels of what we do in music. It really doesn't matter what we do in life. Lives can be touched in profound ways by doing meaningful, soulful things in a committed way.

Lenny is not God, as his sign says. But he certainly is able to evoke a soul from shoes.

What a gift to give through a pair of shoes!

I carry Lenny's card with me....I am naïve enough to believe that his good soulfulness will travel with me.

There is a vitality, a life force, a quickening that is translated through you into action, and there is only one of you in all time, this expression is unique, and if you block it, it will never exist through any other medium; and be lost. The world will not have it. It is not your business to determine how good it is, not how it compares with other expression. It is your business to keep it yours clearly and directly, to keep the channel open. You do not even have to believe in yourself or your work. You have to keep open and aware directly to the urges that motivate you. Keep the channel open. No artist is pleased. There is no satisfaction whatever at any time. There is a queer, divine satisfaction, a blessed unrest that keeps us marching and makes us more alive than the others.

Martha Graham

Musician's Spirit

stories of courage and vision

One of the roles that storying plays is that it can document one's courage in facing life and the courage of others in facing life's challenges. By sharing stories, we are given courage, and perhaps a better understanding of hope and the human spirit as well. All these qualities are necessary for artistic music making.

One of the most inspirational among many stories that I have encountered is the poetry of Mattie Stepanek. Living with a rare form of Muscular Dystrophy, Mattie has lost three siblings to the disease. He lives with the grief of watching his siblings die. Despite the extreme difficulties life has brought him, he writes poetry that speaks beyond his eleven years of age. His poetry writing began at age three as a way of dealing with life, which despite his difficulties, he views as a miracle. Each of his poems is a story unto itself. I have found his poetry simple, direct, honest, tremendously insightful, and even soothing. I cannot recommend his poetry books enough to all readers of this book. If musicians could carry the love that this young man has in his heart, they would understand the music that they perform more profoundly. His poems bring both tears and expanded hearts to all that read them.

Mattie understands the role of storying. His storying is through poetry, which is a powerful vehicle for storying and re-storying. I have chosen two of his poems to share with you. Seek out his books for more. His wisdom and love go far beyond his years. We could all benefit from his stories.

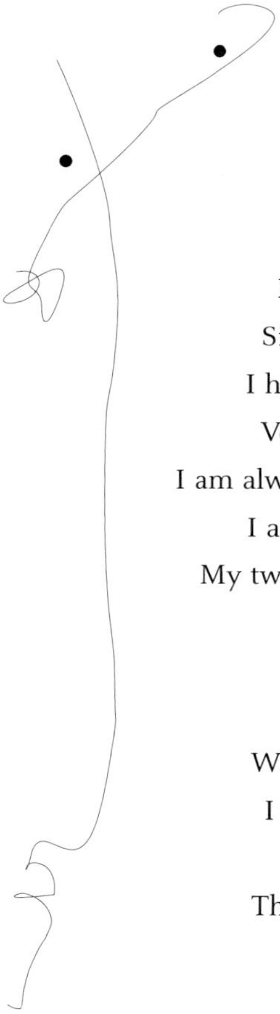

I am Mattie J.T. Stepanek.
My body has light skin,
Red blood, blue eyes, and blond hair.
Since I have mitochondrial myopathy,
I have a trach, a ventilator, and oxygen.
Very poetic, I am, and very smart, too.
I am always brainstorming ideas and stories.
I am a survivor, but someday, I will see
My two brothers and one sister in Heaven.
When I grow up, I plan to become
A father, a writer, a public speaker,
And most of all, a peacemaker.
Whoever I am, and whatever happens,
I will always love my body and mind,
Even if it has different abilities
Than other peoples' bodies and minds.
I will always be happy, because
I will always be me.

May 2001

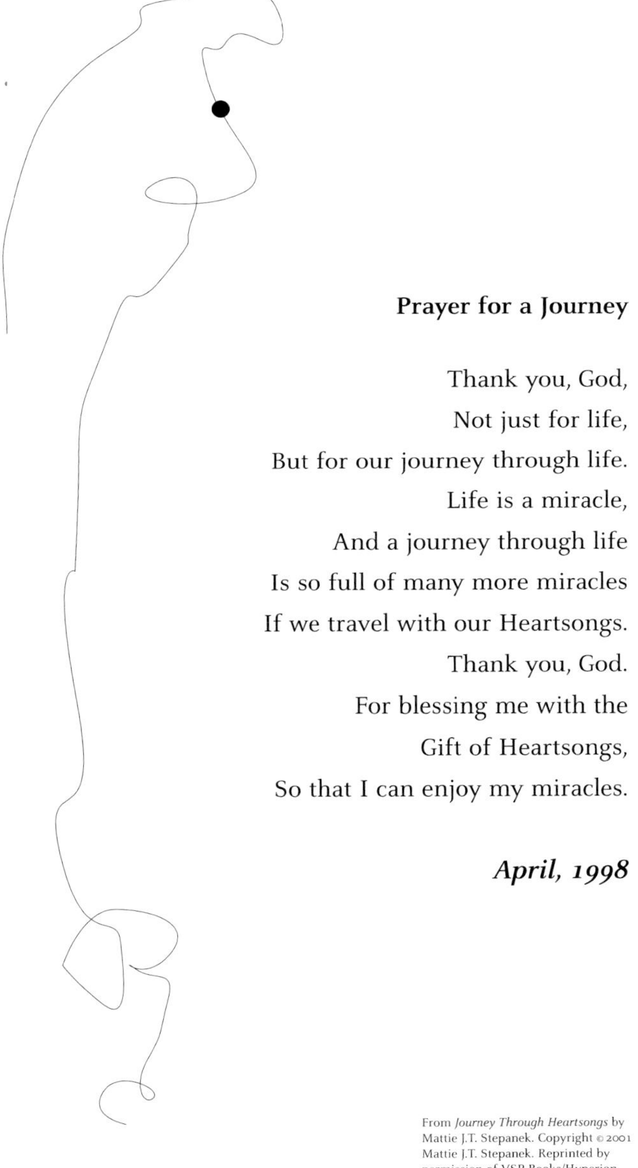

Prayer for a Journey

Thank you, God,
Not just for life,
But for our journey through life.
Life is a miracle,
And a journey through life
Is so full of many more miracles
If we travel with our Heartsongs.
Thank you, God.
For blessing me with the
Gift of Heartsongs,
So that I can enjoy my miracles.

April, 1998

Authors Note: Mattie's books of poetry are listed in the bibliography of this book. They can be purchased through the website www.VSPBooks.com.

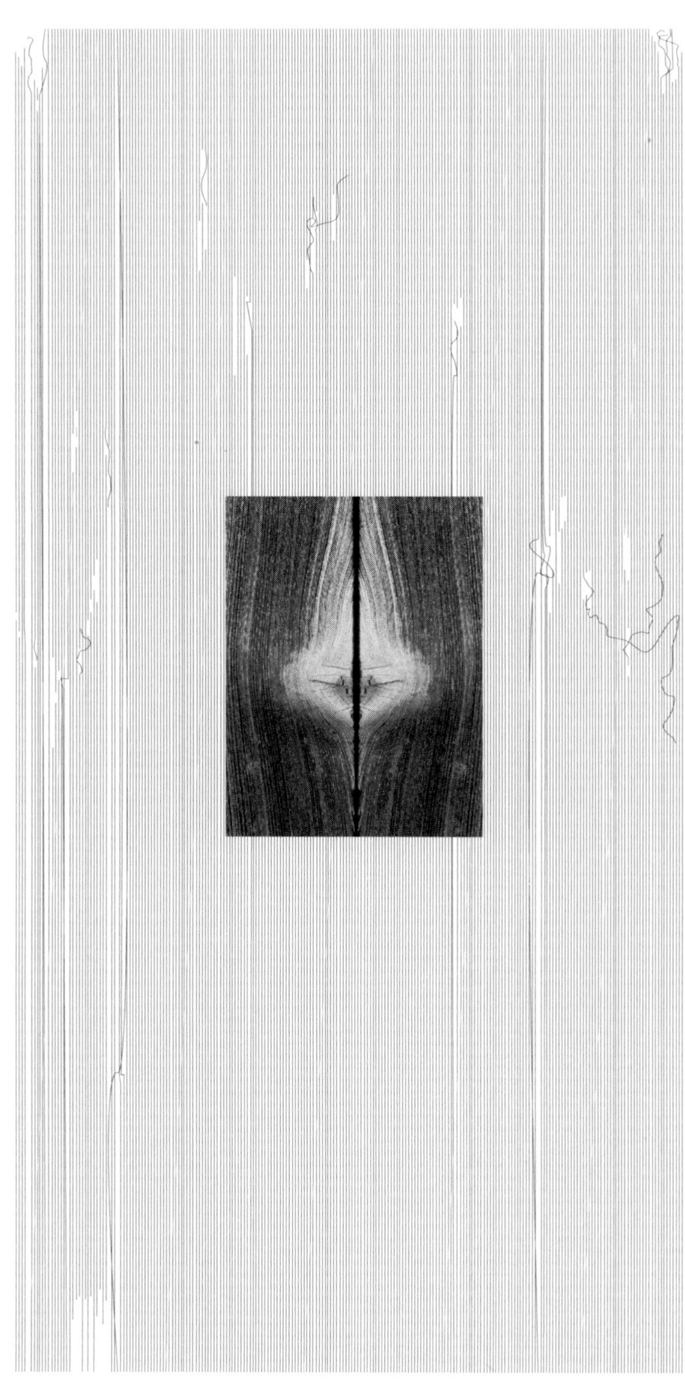

III

listening

Communicating is a practice. You have to be skillful in order to communicate. Good will is not enough. You have to learn how to do it. Maybe you have lost your capacity to listen. Maybe the other person has spoken so often with bitterness, always condemning and blaming, that you have had enough. You cannot listen anymore. You begin to try to avoid him or her. You don't have the capacity to listen to that person anymore. **(p. 91)**

*Loving Speech will rescue us. Compassionate listening will rescue us. This is a miracle performed by us, as practitioners. You have the capacity to do it. You have enough peace, enough compassion and understanding in the depth of your consciousness. You have to call on it for help....***(p. 107)**

Listening with empathy means you listen in such a way that the other person feels you are really listening, really understanding, hearing with your whole being—with your heart. But how many of us can listen like that? **(p. 92)**

Deep Listening is the kind of listening that helps us to keep compassion alive while the other speaks, which may be for half an hour or 45 minutes. During this time you have in mind only one idea, one desire: to listen in order to give the other person the chance to speak and suffer less. **(p. 93)**

Your equipment here is compassion, which can be nourished and kept alive with the practice of mindful breathing. Mindful breathing generates the energy of mindfulness. **(p. 94)**

Thich Naht Hahn

Anger

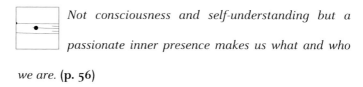

Not consciousness and self-understanding but a passionate inner presence makes us what and who we are. **(p. 56)**

The spiritual life is equivalent to living the poetry of the world, not the facts. **(p. 84)**

Thomas Moore

Original Self

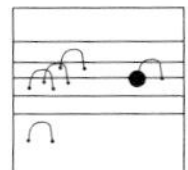

Under every deep, a lower deep opens. **(p.167)**

Ralph Waldo Emerson

Circles

When you are creating a piece of music as a conductor, you are trying to create a family, in a sense. You're trying to diminish them and me and it, and you're trying to bring it all together so it is us. All of it. All in some cohesive, connected, unified way. So the more the nervous system, the vessels—all the things that connect the parts of the body—are more securely developed, it begins to function as effectively as a body, so it is our expression, it is our music; it isn't his music, it isn't their music, it isn't the composers music, it's ours. Kind of like the Father, Son, and Holy Ghost—it's God! (p. 20)

Frank Battisti

Conducting With Feeling by Frederick Harris

I was struck with a remarkable revelation about two years ago. This revelation came as a by-product of some intense thought and pedagogical work on the problem of choral intonation. That work eventually birthed a book on the subject titled *Choral Ensemble Intonation: Methods, Procedures, and Exercises* (GIA, 2000). However, after I developed the pedagogical materials for that text, I began to discover that the secret of in-tune singing was stupendously simple: Listening. But at face value, listening is not what it appears to be. I know that may sound ridiculous, but hear me out.

Before I begin, please remember that as music teachers, conductors, and pedagogues in general, we have not made a conscious effort to teach listening. We have always assumed that listening was a given, because to some extent, we as teachers and performers listen. It is not to be taken for granted for many reasons. Simply stated, the reason choirs, bands, and orchestras do not sing and play in-tune is because they do not listen as *musicians* need to listen. When they enter the rehearsal, they carry their "life ears" into the rehearsal with them. Those ears are conditioned to shield us from the sounds of the outside world. Musicians, unless they are unusually gifted, enter the rehearsal or practice room with the listening skills that they use in the everyday world. This degree and intensity of listening is simply inadequate for the depth of listening required of music-makers.

One must also consider the prioritizing of the senses. (Note: When I speak of senses, I am talking about six senses: sight, smell, hearing taste, touch and *kinesthesia*—your movement sense). Before entering the rehearsal or practice room, the sense of sight is probably the most important of our senses. When musicians enter the rehearsal, their hearing sense should be moved up to priority number one, followed by the sixth sense, which is kinesthesia. All energies must be placed on hearing. Hearing, or rather listening with the whole being, should be the most important operating sense of the musician.

In rehearsal, I think we spend too much time telling people the specifics of what to listen to, i.e. specific notes, rhythms, etc. I believe the first step is to get them to listen to everything. Musicians should listen to everything else except themselves. When one opens one's listening to the larger musical community, musical issues seem to disappear. Music is a communal act in which all of the members of the community must be fully engaged. In addition to being engaged with ones ears and aural sense, listening must take place underneath an umbrella of love and care. When one loves others, one hears what they speak or sing with an inner profoundness that is unmistakable. When a musician profoundly listens in such a way, musical problems seem to disappear.

The problem is much larger than you might imagine. We do not listen in our daily lives. In fact, as we grow older, we listen less and less because the world assaults us from all angles, including our listening sense. We are bombarded by music and incessant media overload. When we do communicate, most of that communication is wordless and occurs via computer on the Internet. Our ears in our modern world are not as important as they once were...our eyes are the most important sense for gaining information. So, if we do nothing to re-set sensual priorities, musicians enter rehearsals listening as they do in everyday life. Such listening skills are totally inadequate for music making.

I recently saw an interview on television involving a man who has been blind since birth. When asked whether his other senses are better than everyone else's, he replied no, simply heightened to an amazing degree. He talked about how he could identify more than 60 different birdcalls. He spoke in depth on how he could ascertain the spirit of a person by their speech because their sibilants gave him a direct link to their soul. I was taken aback by his comments and thought my goodness, if musicians would only listen and hear what he hears!

Well, the fact of the matter is that we must hear with level of acuity and sensitivity. We must also reprioritize our listening to being our number one sense. So how does one reactivate and reprioritize that high level of listening? Once again, perhaps, by story.

By telling stories, persons begin to listen in a more profound and personal way. It is *this* type of listening that musicians desperately need to use in order to make the artistic judgments that they must make. Story causes them to quiet themselves. Story causes them to relate what they hear to their lives. Story is personal, and story can be compelling. To tell stories is human. To tell stories that will open musicians up to listening must be honestly and spontaneously told, and spoken from the heart. There has to be an underlying passion and commitment to those stories. And the stories must be told without fear or embarrassment. Well told stories can cause people to listen to themselves vicariously through the story that is being told. Think of how closely you listened to all the stories of the lives of the people that were affected by the World Trade Center bombings. You listened and connected. Human stories about human life truths will open people up so that they listen with a new sense.

However, you will find that they begin to listen immediately after the story, but do not have the endurance to stay "listening." How does one increase listening endurance? By simply asking the musicians to listen harder, listen to themselves first, then listen to everyone else except themselves. Musicians must make themselves and the clatter of their own cognitive brains less so that they hear the musical world at large more. They must listen with both and the inward and outward ear, but hear all others first.

How does one acquire and practice this skill? By listening to *life.* Work hard to hear every word of every conversation. Concentrate to hear the subtleties in each word as a person speaks them. Listen for human emotion in sentences. Listen and hear every sound in the world, and be humble when doing so. I've learned that when people understand and use humbleness, they hear with more internal depth.

Go and listen to nature. There is a whole world of subtle sounds on which to practice. Do Yoga and listen to your own breath. Read poetry and *hear* what it has to say to you. Look at great art and listen to how it speaks loudly in its almost silent language. Read every word of books you read. Let listening enrich your life. When you does all or part of the above, your musical life will deepen.

I also believe that a profound sense of listening can only be accessed through awe and a profound sense of wonder for the art we create. When we are in a state of awe, we hear better, more profoundly, more inwardly. In the words of Abraham Joshua Heschel, what we cannot comprehend by analysis, we become aware of by awe. Or if I may paraphrase, what we cannot hear by analysis, we may hear more deeply through awe and wonder.

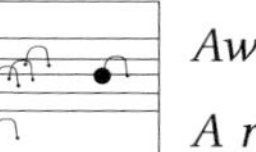

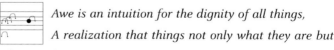

Awe is an intuition for the dignity of all things,
A realization that things not only what they are but also stand, However remotely,
For something supreme. **(p. 3)**

Abraham Joshua Heschel

I Asked for Wonder

By placing one's own self in a place of awe and wonder, we revisit the place where, as children, we heard all. Children hear *all.* Have you noticed that? They hear every word of every conversation. Why? Because their very existence depends on their ability to hear and listen. Musicians seem to dwell on the edge of awe and wonder, but seldom enter into it, and when they do, few actually stay. They become almost insensitive to wonder because the world they live in is insensitive to it. They live on the edge of their musical fantasy, denying themselves the leap that will change their world. To exist in this world is to exist in a world of brilliant colors of sound and human emotions. To deny this world is to live in a darkened world, a world with no colors and only passing grays. Life and music is in black and white. We often pray in similarly dark places.

Musicians need to reawaken their natural sense of hearing, then connect it with their intuition, which is open, non-judgmental, and always performed from a loving place. We must view listening as a miracle; a miracle that will provide all that is necessary for us to live the music we perform.

I also believe that awe and wonder are accessed through the door of silence and quiet. Surrender to stillness. Give up the controls placed upon you by an external world so that you can listen. In that quiet, we unknowingly mingle with the divine *within* ourselves. This access is simple unless we feed our minds with presumptions and conceit, cling to duplicity, and refuse to *mean what we sense.* After all, hearing is sensation; we need only to hear our own hearing, then think what we feel. We also need to let insight be and listen to the soul's recessed certainty of its being. This idea can be compared to the way you listen to people you love. If we listen in that same way to the music we love, we will hear a whole new world and be immersed in it.

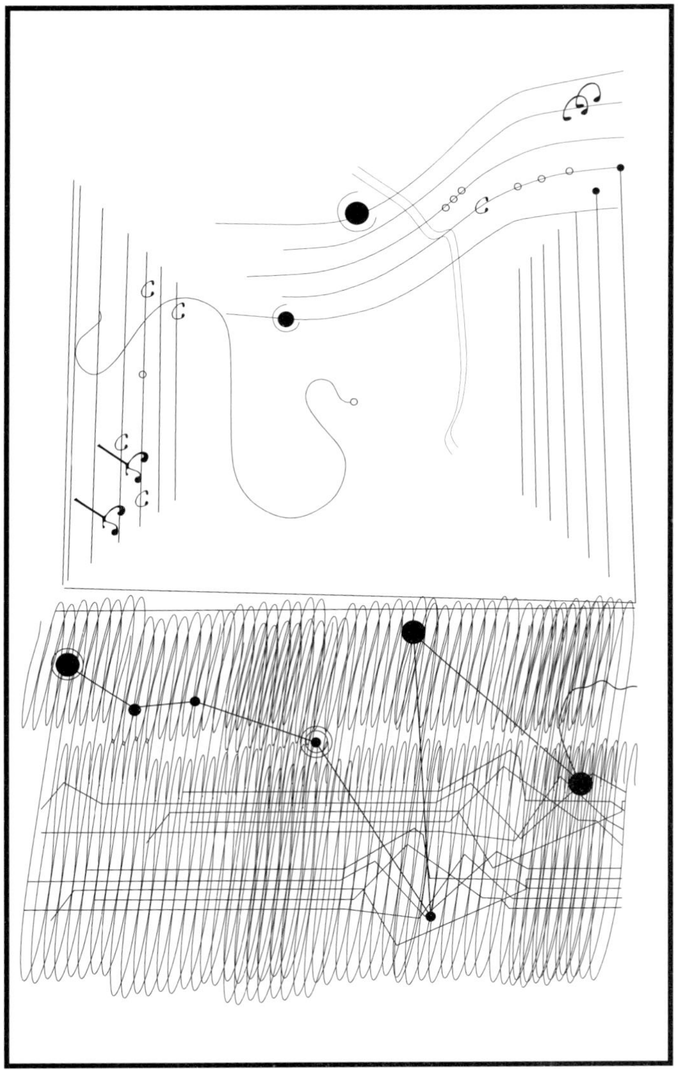

Author Note: I would highly recommend that readers investigate in great detail the book by Thich Naht Hahn entitled *Anger* listed in the bibliography of this book. This book contains an incredible appendix that details how one can lead oneself through the process of being mindful through a series of guided meditations.

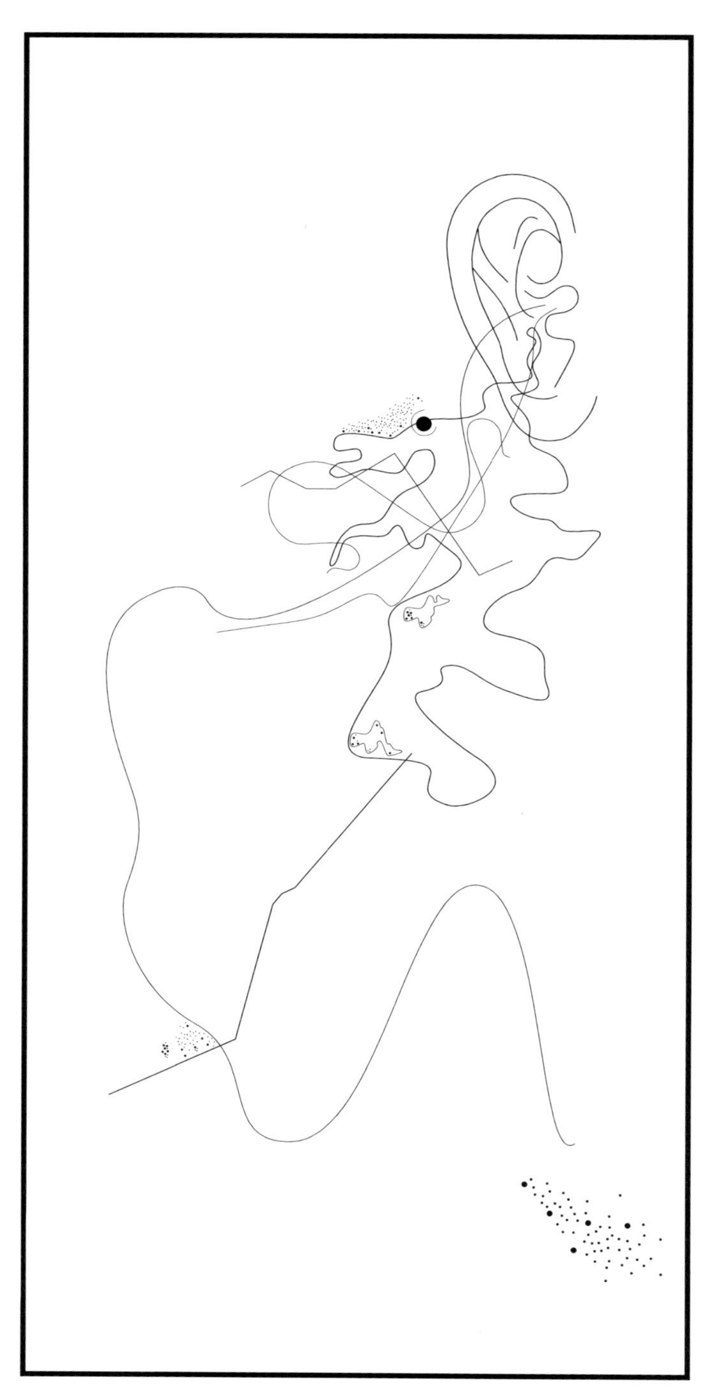

to hear again

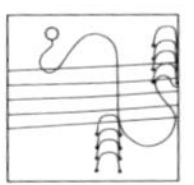

Ah Music, a magic above all that we do here!

Albus Dumbledore, Headmaster of Hogwarts School Of Witchcraft and Wizardry

Harry Potter and The Sorcerer's Stone
by J.K. Rowling

I lost the ability to hear in my right ear at age 19.

In its place now sits a powerful white noise, like the sound of a hundred voices shushing, imploring me to remain still and quiet. It was a devastating loss to me as a musician, a singer, and an aspiring conductor. But mostly, it was a loss to my humanity. I lost much of my ability to communicate with others and respond to the vibrant sounds around me. Reclusive, with my self-confidence and faith fading into the dark shadow of my former self, I spent the next year deep in depression, steeped in questions I could no longer answer.

Music, in all of the ways that I had understood it, had become incomprehensible to me. In my rapidly closing heart, I mourned its death. My body, mind, and spirit warned many times in different ways that I needed to slow down, stop the constant spinning and busy-ness, and that I couldn't do everything. Ironically, yet very poignantly, it was only when I was struck deaf that I finally began to listen and to hear the hurting voices inside. My deafness brought me face to face with both my life and my music and forced me to respond directly to their questions.

Turning my listening inward for the first time, I began to seek out meditation retreats; the first one for three days and the next several for ten days each. For ten hours each day for the first three days I focused my entire attention to the movement of the breath. I had never been still for so long and my body throbbed in aches and pains. The shushing noise swelled in my head and would not let me stay long though, beckoning me to wander away to any thought or image that would provide momentary comfort.

On the third day, exhausted and aching yet still persevering, my mind slowly began to stop its clatter and came to rest. In this stillness, I experienced my own breath for the first time. It was gentle as the ebb and flow of the ocean freed me from the tension and force of my lifestyle. My breathing became like a fine musical phrase with its contoured ascent and gentle decline. Each inspiration became an opportunity to center deeply, each expiration a setting free. I felt my entire body breathe until the breath breathed right through me. After so many years as a singer working with breathing, I had never truly perceived or experienced it. I stood in awe of the clarity and depth of its peaceful, shimmering movement.

For the next seven days each subtle tide allowed built up tensions to flow and dissolve away. As the tensions arose and came to the surface of my body, I was shown in my mind's eye how I had created such tension in my life. I was given a second chance to react with a balanced mind, to react with love and compassion instead of jealousy, anger, or grasping. One by one in rapid succession I was shown the painful images that shaped my contracted sense of self. I saw myself abusing my body, using my mind and spirit like a machine in pursuit of materialism, success, and achievement. My chase had led me only to a greater sense of isolation and loneliness. Soulless pursuits led my spirit to finally stop me and silence me in the only way it knew how: by taking away my ability to hear. Unable to hear, I was forced to relearn how to listen—to my body, to my soul, and to my spirit.

I grounded myself in the very center of my body, mind, and spirit, and my entire being wept. Each painful bodily sensation, each haunting image and anguished emotion, offered me a chance to bring a loving attention to all of the dark and ignored corners of my life. Each aspect asked for my love and my acceptance over and over again until at last I surrendered and a still silence overcame me. My weeping faded and a glowing warmth surrounded me. Out of the warmth came my own whispered voice: "Can you love all of this, even now?" The slow answer that arose affirmed the gentle release of my held breath. Each teardrop sounded the bell of a peaceful, joyous heart.

Can we learn to know and love ourselves more deeply, more intimately? Will we choose to be defined by our perceived limitations and boundaries, or will we choose to grow beyond them, relinquishing our deeply held, limiting beliefs and fears?

In my loss, I traded a false sense of mastery for a genuine experience of the mystery, which permeates every facet of spiritual and musical life; a life of wisdom that cannot be traded for any skill. It is this wisdom in our lives and in our music that allows us to experience the greater mystery, the great music of life itself.

Dominic Gregorio

2 December 2001

Dominic Gregorio lives in Guelph, Ontario, Canada.

9/11/01

A terrorist is the product of our education that says that fantasy is not real, that says that aesthetics is just for artists, that says that soul is only for priests, imagination is trivial or dangerous and for crazies, and that reality, what we must adapt to, is the external world, and that world is dead. A terrorist is the result of this whole long process of wiping out the psyche. Corbin said to me one time, 'What is wrong with the Islamic world is that it has destroyed its images, and without these images that are so rich and so full of tradition, they are going crazy because they have no containers for their imaginative power?' **(p. 187)**

James Hillman

A Blue Fire

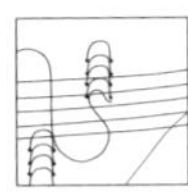

In spite of everything, I believe that people are good at heart.

Anne Frank

New City

Stanley Kunitz, 95,
new poet laureate,
asked by Elizabeth Farnsworth,
Your success? Your longevity?
replied, I refuse to forget.
I never live in the present only.
I live in all my life at once.

I, knowing already how
to live in space,
learned then to live in time,
both whole and broken.
Old with past and future,
we shall be towers now, and rubble,
memorial and new city, all at once.

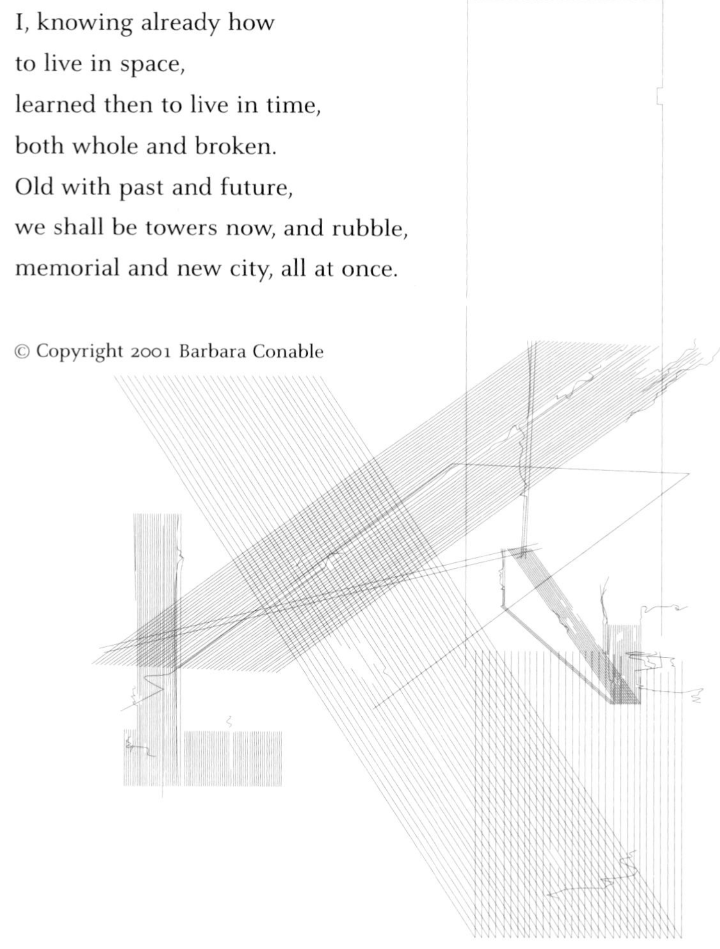

We live in lean times; I know that and I know that you know that. There is a sense of urgency, even of despair, in the air, and we live under the threat of a cloud. Fear and caution abound, and you and I wonder what we can do. Life is harsh and unfair, and judgment swift and arbitrary. The rabbis tell us when a wise man heard that the end of the world was near he went into his garden and planted a tree, an act of courage, audacity and hope—the only possible response. Perhaps it is John Wesley to whom we must turn, who, in times not dissimilar to our own, and on behalf of the cautious to the question, " But what can I do for the kingdom?" he replied:

Do all the good you can,
By all the means you can,
In all the ways you can,
In all the places you can,
At all the times you can,
To all the people you can,
As long as you ever can. **(p. 204)**

Peter Gomes

Sermons

Two strangers in The World Trade Center Tower carry a woman down sixty-two floors in her wheelchair to safety. Daycare caregivers place children in shopping carts and rush them to safety amid smoke, dust, and falling debris and bodies. **A New York Firefighter is filling out retirement papers at Precinct headquarters when the call comes in about World Trade Center One. He rushes out the door, never to be seen again.**

The firefighters' Chaplain is killed as he tries to help a fireman by aiding him and giving him last rights. He took off his helmet to be closer to a firefighter. Father Mike was killed because he removed his helmet and was killed by falling debris. The fireman lovingly carried him back to the friary, laid him at the altar, and returned to Ground Zero.

Innocent victims called home to love ones on cell phones to let them know one of the most important things in life: that they love them and always will. Love and loving ends up being the only rational act on a day of irrationality. **Dave Tarrentino lowered himself into a fire hole in The Pentagon to save the life of a man on fire at his office desk.**

Abe Zolmaniwicz, a Jew, had a Christian friend who was wheelchair bound. They both came to work that day to work on the 62nd floor, as they had done for years. Both men were the best of friends. Abe, on the 62nd floor, told the wheelchair bound man's caretaker who brought him to work that day to leave and get to safety and he would care for his friend. They used the phones to call their loved ones. They decided to die together. Both perished by each other's side. Love, friendship, and human care carried them to the next world as the building collapsed on them.

Timothy Pearson was helping people escape when the building collapsed on him. A hand reached through a hole with a flashlight; he said, "Hold on." He was pulled from the rubble to safety by the hand with the flashlight. The man disappeared to help others. Timothy does not know who this was, but refers to him as his "light angel."

. . . .
. . . .
. . . .
. . . .
. . . .
. . . .

Two office workers a woman never knew carry her down 69 flights of stairs in a wheelchair. To this day, she does not know who saved her life. A seeing-eye dog leads its owner down 64 floors to safety.

. . . .
. . . .
. . . .
. . . .
. . . .
. . . .
. . . .
. . . .
. . . .
. . . .
. . . .

The role of music and the arts changed forever on September 11th. On that day, we all closed a bit more, and looked behind us a bit more. The easygoing daily pace of our lives is gone forever. Everyone's life was changed on that day.

The role of the artist in this new world changed dramatically as a result of the terrorist acts upon our spirits and our souls. I have thought much about its impact upon me, and the people in my life, including the choir I conduct on a daily basis. If there ever was a time where music and art in general was more important, it is now.

Because of an act of tremendous inhumanity, great acts of humanity have been manifested and will continue to be manifested. We hear of incredible acts of heroism and human compassion. But for those of us not at Ground Zero, the impact is more substantial than we would like to acknowledge. I heard William Sloan Coffin, the great American Preacher, once say that when the world got crazy, it was only through music and art that he could again make sense of the world.

We must realize that people who create music are more spiritually closed now than they were prior to September 11th. We have, perhaps unknowingly, erected a protective shell around our spirits and ourselves. All this has numbed many of us, including our students. We must use our art to maintain and re-establish contact with the world. One of the ways that contact can be re-established is through the music we create.

Music can provide the magic that *Harry Potter* represents. In a sense, we have all become orphans and wish we could resort to magic to soothe our wounds. Is it any wonder that millions of people are flocking to see this picture? People are flocking to see this picture just as people flocked to see *The Wizard of Oz* during the Great Depression. *Harry*

Potter and J.K. Rowling offer hope to all that see the movie. Harry is told in the middle of the movie that he needs to be careful. "Never spend so much time dreaming that you forget to live your life."

This book is about connection, or perhaps, reconnection through music. We should not forget that music is our medium of connection to the world at large. Our world is a different place now, and we must realize that people we work with who make music with us may have to be reminded that the events of September 11th *have* affected their ability to sing or play because it has impaired their ability to be open.

This book is about story and the pivotal roles that narrative can play in finding resonant places from life that can make music come alive. Therefore, it is story that can draw us out of our collective stupor and collective fear. Reading stories of tremendous heroism and humanity can begin the process. Each day in *The New York Times,* life "stories" of all those who have perished are published and are available at www.nytimes.com. Those pages place stories with faces; for each face is part of a life story. *The Times,* in its wisdom, understands this, and has placed a human face on this tragedy. Those stories touched my heart, and I cry every morning when reading them. Stories, *their* stories, help me to process these horrendous events.

And process them I must. As musicians, we must continue to bring clarity to the world through our art. Acknowledging the closure of spirit and identifying the closure can only restore that distinct clarity of our spirits and storying to bring newfound depth to the music we make. For if music is a human art, only when our humanity is restored will our music speak to others.

Remind those you teach that while the world requires this "insulation" of the soul, we must fight to remain open so that our individual voices are not also victims of September 11th. In addition to storying, love and care go a great distance toward those ends. The world is now a different place. Acknowledge what it has done to all of us. Also acknowledge that our art can help mend and repair the distrust and hate that the event brought upon us all. To sing and play better now than we did before September 11th is probably the best tribute to those who gave of their lives. Beauty and art that is birthed out of love can be a powerful weapon against this new enemy of humankind.

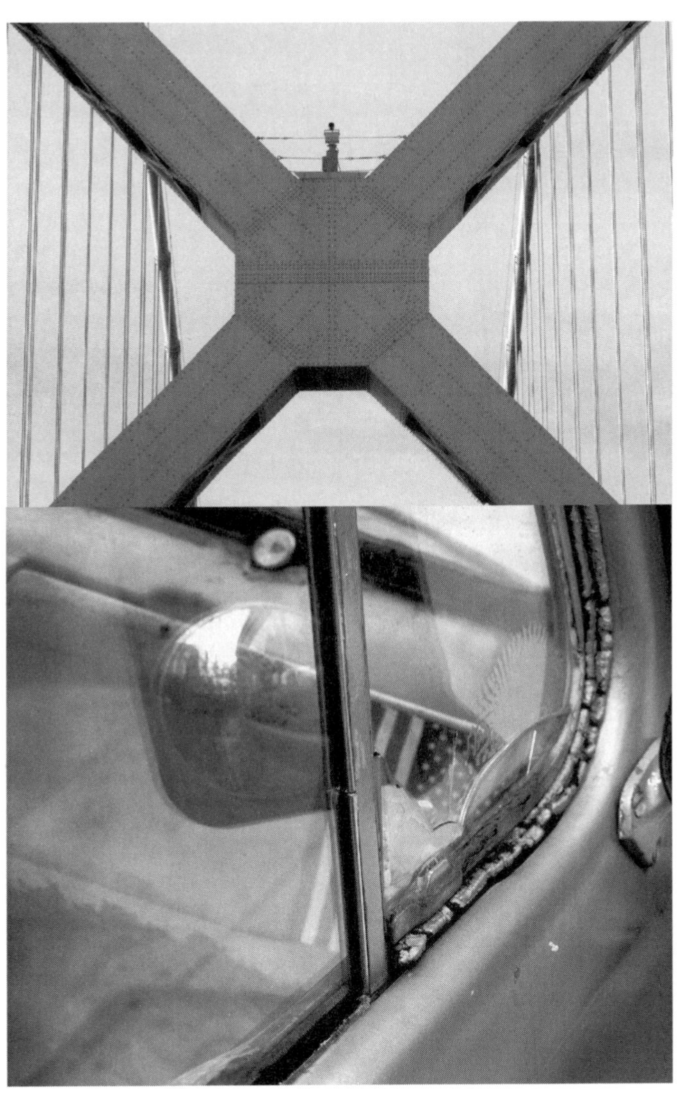

prayers before sleep

Author's Note: It is often difficult to find the right place to journey to when a piece requires deep spirituality and simplicity. What follows is one of the stories I had forgotten about in my childhood. It is only since I became aware of the role of story that I went searching for my appropriate life experience. I suspect that each of you has similar stories from childhood; perhaps hundreds that would assist in your music making.

As best as I can remember, between the ages of 2 and 5, I received a bath each night before I went to bed. Thinking back, I can remember much about them. The big-footed white enamel tub, playing in the water, and the suds. The smell of Calgon water softener!

After my bath, my mom would dry me off, and I would get into my flannel pajamas. I can always remember how I loved the soft feeling of them. My mom would also comb my hair. Boy, did I love that feeling. The long-tooth comb brushing up against my forehead was such a great sensation.

After combing my hair, Mom would take me into the bedroom, and we would both kneel down and I would say my prayers. Sometimes we would pray out loud, and sometimes quietly. As I got older, I prayed quietly. It is not the feeling of the prayers that I remember, but I do remember the feeling of praying! I can honestly say that it was the most open, most innocent time of my entire life. It was a quiet time in my day; a time for Mom and I to kneel together and to talk to God. In looking back, I can remember what I prayed for. My mom always taught me to pray for others, and I never prayed for myself or for things. I would wish for wellness and good health on all those I loved. And, in addition to praying, it was quiet time with my mom; a woman who was and is so generous of spirit to everyone. Those prayers before sleep did much to build what I now realize is my spiritual core. It is such a good feeling to revive those feelings when they can benefit the music.

What fascinates me now is how I had forgotten about that beautiful experience of childhood over the years! How does that happen to us? Part of the reason is because we are always "living in the moment," those moments push such simple life events to the recesses of our minds. Part of the reason, also, is that I have not spent enough time with myself to quiet the "in the moment" noise to take journeys into the early parts of my life that gave me such joy and taught me such important lessons. Events of childhood life are profoundly influential. They are loaded with story, and they are loaded with life and its connected feelings. For it is the feelings that one needs to be in touch with as a musician.

What is even more exciting is that last night, before I went to bed, I knelt down and said my prayers again after 40 years of life. It felt so good to connect with myself again in that way, and it felt the same as it did then. I cannot wait to use that feeling when it is appropriate on a piece that requires me to be in such a simple, vulnerable place.

The only thing missing last night was that there was no one around to comb my hair.

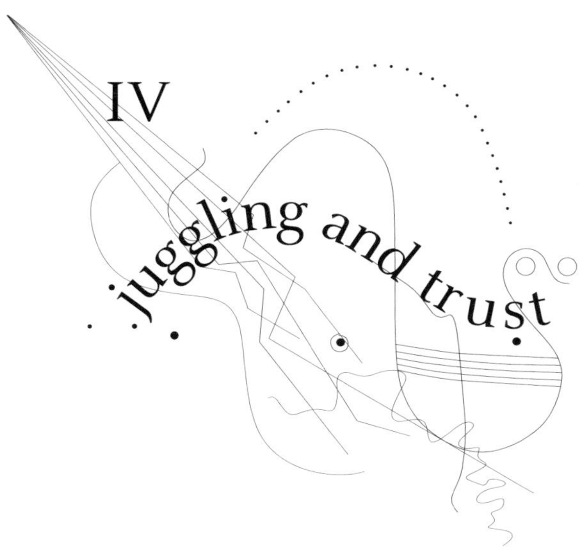

IV

juggling and trust

Authors Note: This article, written by Father Carlos Urrutigoity, is reprinted from the newsletter of The Society of St. John. Nicholas Beck, a Westminster student who was a member of this trip, brought this article to my attention. In a world where we take so much for granted, including the music we make, a story like this causes us to decide what is most important in our lives, and also to believe in the goodness of others. This article is not about a trip, but it documents the out-of-ordinary activity of a group of high school young men, which is Juggling, and how that activity was the vehicle for them believing in themselves. Juggling, just as music is for musicians, was simply the chosen mode of transportation for this soulful journey. When one trusts themselves and others, miracles happen on a daily basis.

The connection between our faith and Europe, however can be somewhat—since so much of what we associate with Europe (kings, cathedrals, class, and nobility)—contrary to how America defines itself. While America is undeniably the child of Europe, from the beginning it was a rebellious child that had repudiated the traditions of her parents. The traditions of Europe were all informed by the Catholic faith, even if in a remote way. This fact stands, whether we like it or not, because Europe, once called Christendom, grew out of this faith. One needs only to make a brief survey of art history to verify this. The Englishmen who settled America were already a people estranged from their beginnings by their adherence to the Protestant or Anglican faiths. This distance was increased when they revolted against their king and formed their own country. Now we live in a futuristic world of stealth bombers, the Internet, and fast food. How far we have come from the people who built cathedrals, went on pilgrimages, and fought each other with swords and shields. The world we live in now bears no apparent resemblance or connection to the world out of which it rose so long ago. Nevertheless, an inescapable bond exists. I wish to tell a story of a recent adventure that illustrates that bond: a dozen American teenagers bicycling the most venerable road to the sanctuary of St. James, a symbol of the old faith.

The boys and the teacher who leads them are all members of St. Gregory's Juggling Troupe and have been performing around Scranton, Pennsylvania, for over two years. During the lunch break of a juggling workshop in Philadelphia, they conceived the idea to juggle and sing across Europe like their peers in the Middle Ages. They thought how glorious it would be to bring no money for food or lodging—only a return plane ticket, forcing them to make their way across Europe of the faith in absolute and immediate dependence on Providence. The more they talked about the idea, the more serious they became, and soon were planning the trip in earnest. They began raising money by washing cars, selling T-shirts, working on farms, selling candy bars, and

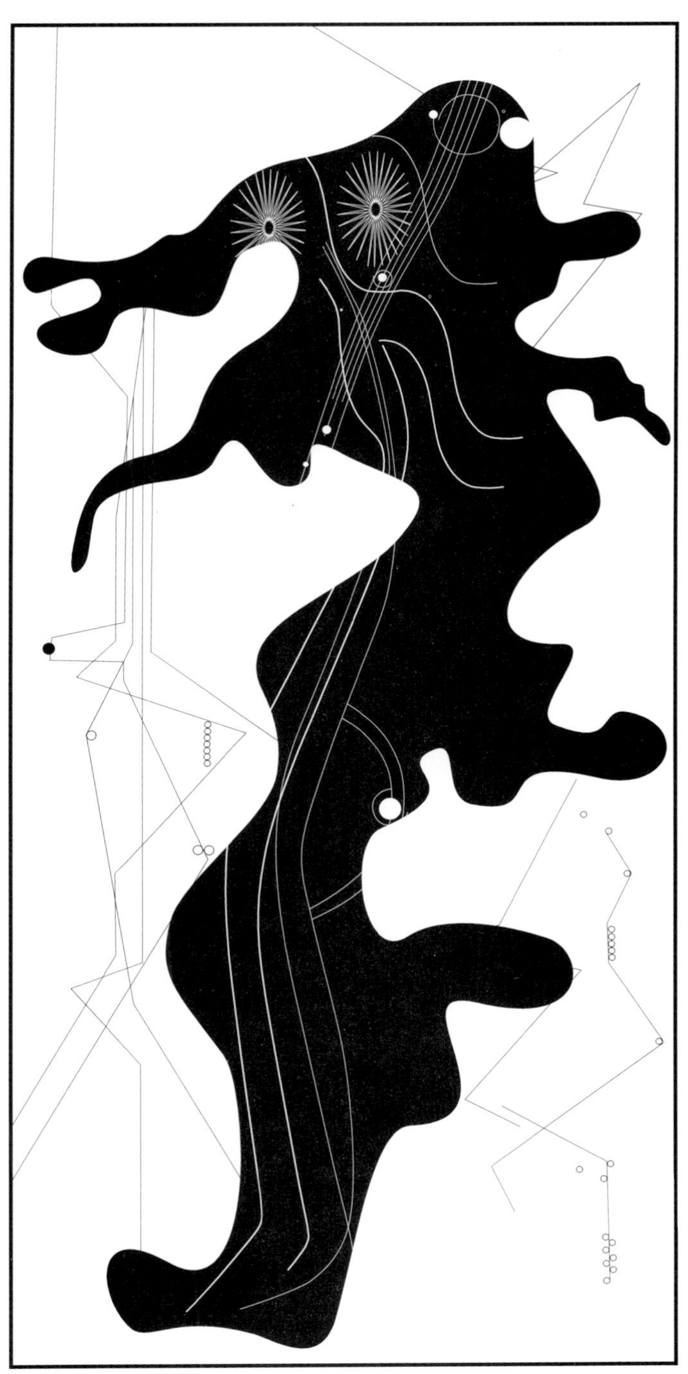

simply begging people to give them money. Soon, enough money was coming in that they started believing their madcap idea might actually work. Now they had to come up with a clear destination and travel route. They decided to make a pilgrimage to Santiago de Compostela in Spain, the burial place of the Apostle James, and the greatest center of pilgrimage after Jerusalem.

Next they needed to decide the means of travel. Walking to Santiago was too slow, car riding was too fast and easy, and the train was both too expensive and presented no challenge. Only one option remained: the bicycle. Most of them either had or could borrow a bike, and none seemed to mind that they would be adding a few more obstacles to an already difficult trip. How were they to transport their bikes? What would they do if there was a serious breakdown? How would they find the energy to juggle after biking many miles in the hot Spanish sun? These questions were impossible to answer without going over there and finding out. They bought round-trip plane tickets to Paris, packed up their bikes, and were off. Upon their arrival, they juggled for a day in front of Notre Dame Cathedral, a joyful beginning to their wondrous adventure.

Each day they woke up, usually in fields by the road, wondering when they would eat next or where they would sleep. How would they make the next 40 kilometers without breakfast or lunch? To their great relief and delight they discovered again and again enough money to not only survive, but to eat well. They ate a variation of the same meal every day—a loaf of bread per person filled with cheese, meat, and olives if they were rich, juice in the afternoon and wine in the evening. They would sit down to these meals sweating with the glory of yet another successful show—hungry beyond belief, and thankful for the miracle of once again finding

Musician's Spirit

enough food to eat. Drinking long draughts of cheap Spanish wine, they would sit musing on their wonderful feasts made from songs and juggling balls flying high in the air.

There were times when they were very hungry in cities where the police strictly forbade performing. It was then that they thanked God or the devil for their ignorance of the Spanish tongue. After playing the dumb foreigner, they turned the corner and performed again until it was time to resume the role. Once, after biking enough kilometers to make them ravenous, they arrived in Puente la Reina with plenty of songs to sing and clubs to juggle, but no audience. Finally, a young girl came to the rescue, showing them how to survive. "Juggle here," she said as she pointed to the empty courtyard of an apartment complex. Tired and hungry enough to try anything, they did as they were told. They began their show, singing and juggling for no one. Soon, however, a window opened, and then another and another, until the whole building had sprouted eyes—and coins, bills, and food were being tossed down into the grinning mouths of their waiting hats.

I am writing of this event not only because it is an inspirational story when viewed through the eye of mass culture, but also because it represents a historical reality. A group of boys from Moscow, Pennsylvania, in the year 1999, unwittingly recreated the spirit of the Middle Ages by traveling to Europe and, with no money, juggled and sang their way along one of the oldest Catholic pilgrimage routes. This kind of trip had to take place in Europe; for Europe is at home with pilgrims and jugglers and Franciscan-type fools. Even if people had rejected them, the fountains and cathedrals would still cry: "Welcome, juggle and sing for us!" Americans flock to old Europe in droves every year. Perhaps it is only to eat, drink, and find romance, but then why Europe—why not Africa or Asia? It is because our roots and the secret juices of our very being lie buried in this land. Americans are traveling back to the place from which they began. How natural that our hearts and guts long for the land that gave us a conquering spirit, the source of our being. To rediscover its own identity, America must understand its origins. To determine the course of its future, it must reexamine its place in relation to these origins. The tale of this pilgrimage is but a sign of our need to rediscover the God of our old faith, the God that makes all things new.

For those interested, the Jugglers of St. Gregory's Academy are available for performances, and make this trip each year. They rely solely on juggling events and donations to support their trips. For those interested in making a donation to their cause, contact:

St. Gregory's Academy
RR8, Box 8214
Moscow, PA 18444
(570)-842-8112

a visit to St. Gregory's

For the rest of my life, I want to reflect on what light is. (p. 153)

Albert Einstein

Quantum Theology

To understand soul, we cannot turn to science for a definition. Its meaning is best given by its context. The root metaphor of the analyst's point of view is that behavior is understandable because it has inside meaning. The inside meaning is suffered and experienced. Other words long associated with the word soul amplify it further: mind, spirit, heart, life, warmth, humanness, personality, individuality, intentionality, essence, innermost, purpose, emotion, quality, virtue, morality, sin, wisdom, death, God. A soul is said to be 'troubled,' 'old,' 'disembodied,' 'immortal,' 'lost,' 'innocent,' 'inspired.' (p. 20)

James Hillman

A Blue Fire

One of my students who had just completed his first year at the Choir College invited me to visit his former school. This student was one of those students in your choir who you do not easily forget. A vital spirit every rehearsal, he would have made a mark on anyone who came in contact with him. He possessed a remarkable ability to connect to the music. Upon talking with him, one sensed an immediate openness and honesty quite unlike many persons of his age. He was an older student who delayed attending a four-year college in lieu of other experiences. While the three years certainly make a difference, the aliveness in this young man certainly sets him apart.

At the end of the school year, I was taking my daughter to an away soccer tournament. This tournament happened to be in the area of this student's former boarding school. I received an e-mail almost every day checking as to whether I could come and visit the school.

His gentle insistence coupled with his enthusiasm prompted my curiosity. "So tell me about St. Gregory's," I asked. "Well, it's a small school; 60 boarding boys, ages 9–12. It was founded by an order of priests who were propagating the Latin Mass." I asked him how he heard about the school. "Through the magazine *Latin Mass*," he replied. I was a bit taken aback.

I had heard from other students and had learned first-hand of this student's love for Chant and all things Latin. In fact, he had exquisitely coached six of the men in the choir this year to sing the entire Ubi caritas chant without a conductor. The singing was done with incredible artistry and honesty. At the time, I thought nothing of it other than the work of some very fine young musicians.

When I arrived at the tournament, I gave this student a call to set up a "tour." We agreed on time and place. In the meantime, I conjured up idyllic images of a luxurious private school with rolling green lawns and well-manicured facilities.

James Jordan

The student picked me up and we drove about twenty minutes outside one of the cities in the Northeast. The area was nothing to speak of; in fact, it was a bit depressed. No elegant estates, just small homes that had seen better days. We rounded a corner where I saw the sign "St. Gregory's Academy." I glanced up the hill. Not what I had envisioned.

We passed the headmasters house; it was just that, a house. We continued up the dirt road to the main building. I looked for other buildings; there were none.

"What was this before it was a school?" I asked. "It was an orphanage and then later it was a retreat house for the diocese. Then I think the order bought it and began the school."

We pulled up to the front door. We passed through doors that reminded me of the doors that were on the ACME store I shopped in with my parents as a child. There were not many people around. The place was rather non-descript. While clean, it was rather dingy. Floors were slightly dirty, furniture in classrooms was just bare essentials; but I was struck immediately by one fact. I saw a place that was dingy and a bit worn. It had no modern bells and whistles; in fact, many of the sections were in disrepair. However, as this young man showed me around, you might have believed that he was showing me around the most beautiful of mansions. The excitement of showing me this place, for some reason, was so special to him. He took me from dingy classroom to dingy classroom. "In this lounge we had Physics class my senior year." *In this room*? I muttered to myself.

"Is there a Chapel?" I asked. "Oh yes," he said happily, "It is where I sang Mass this morning." Up another dingy flight of steps, and he opened the door. I couldn't believe it. It was a stunningly beautiful Chapel, awash with the smell of incense. Light streaming through beautiful leaded stained glass windows. The space was even more beautiful because of the contrast with the rest of the building. Upon entering, he blessed himself with holy water and genuflected. As a Catholic, I knew I should do it too, but felt awkward. (Why?)

We spent a few quiet moment and then left. We headed down the stairs. "The athletic fields are this direction," he told me. We walked a few yards to a cleared field. It had two soccer goals at either end, with one of the most unusual water towers I have ever seen. It was an octagonal brick tower encircled with windows at the top, capped with a cupola. At the base, the door to the tower was stone, almost castle-like. I looked for the moat!

"Isn't this beautiful?" he asked. To me, it was a below-average athletic field. To him, it was a beautiful place filled with memories. We walked that field quietly for awhile, and then it all began to make sense.

Lessons for teaching are all around us. I was experiencing one of the dying places where spirituality was more important than things; where young men are grown from the inside out; where the history and roots of one's own spirituality is not forgotten. *My God,* I thought. *I am in a place where spirituality is the most important aspect of education.*

At that moment, this place looked beautiful to me, too. I began to feel why it was such an important place. The symbolism of the Chapel became very powerful. It was the most beautiful room for the most important thing...spiritual life.

I am now intensely envious of this young man. For I feel he knows spirituality deeper than I do, because he enjoyed an education that was spiritual and obviously nurtured by love. His love of Gregorian chants and love of the simple direct things gave this young man an incredible spiritual lucidity and human clarity. The school had little money; but they clearly had an incredible mission. They do not need money to educate these boys. They are giving the gift of spirituality. What greater gift can one give?

As we left, he asked me if I liked the place. "I love it....you are very fortunate to have gone to school here." I told him. He replied, "Thank you for coming to see *our* school."

It is very strange. Walking into that place changed me. It reaffirmed that the place where we do our art is not of consequence. It is the spirit and love that fills the place that makes for one's human education. This young man will do remarkable work in the world and will touch many lives because he came from a place that valued spirituality as the core of the educational experience.

We should all be so lucky.

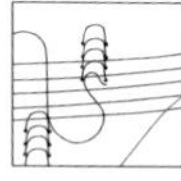

The essence of religion is to see the sublime and the awesome in the Lowliest of things. **(p. 140)**

Thomas Moore

Original Self

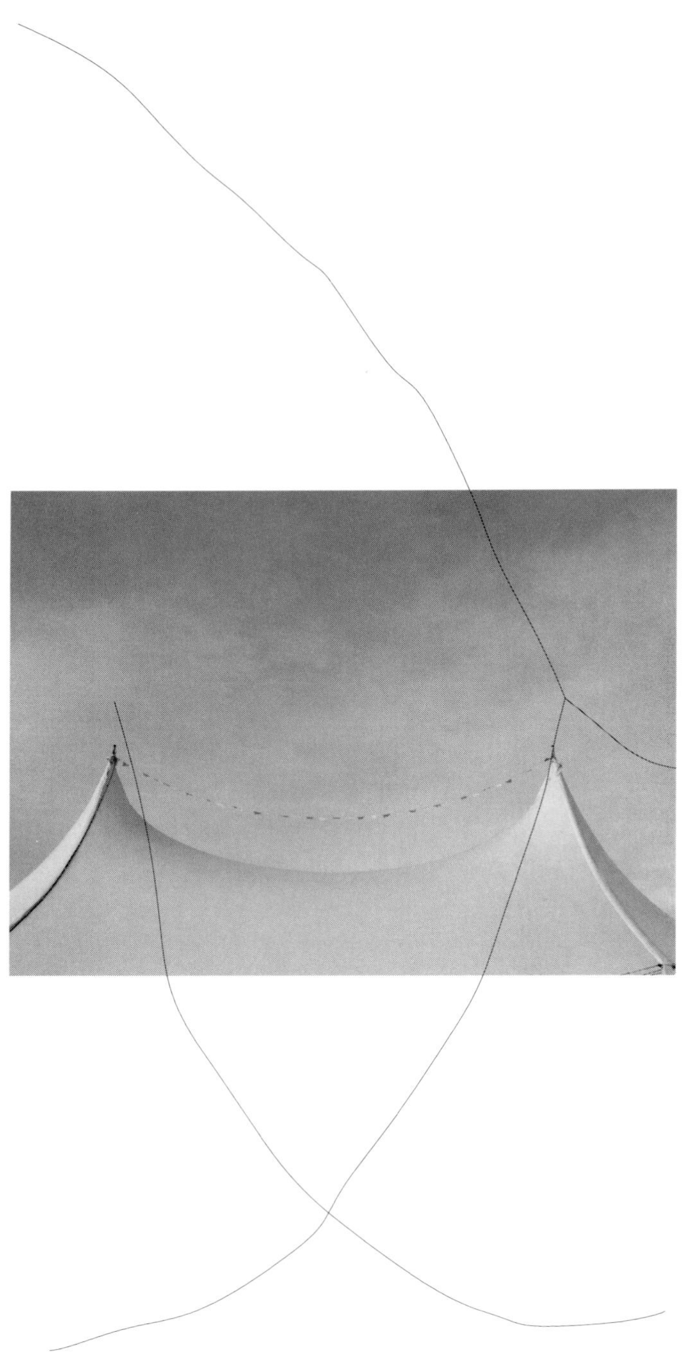

James Jordan

Ever since there have been men, man has given himself over to too little joy. That alone, my brothers, is our original sin. I should believe only in a God who understood how to dance.

Henri Matisse

We hardly ever realize that we can cut anything out of our lives, anytime, in the blink of an eye.

Human beings are perceivers, but the world they perceive is an illusion, an illusion created by the description that was told to them from the moment they were born. So, in essence, the world that their reason wants to sustain is the world created by a description and its dogmatic and inviolable rules, which their reason learns to accept and defend.

Carlos Castaneda

The Wheel of Time

I have one life and one chance to make it count for something....I'm free to choose what that something is, and the something I've chosen is my faith. Now, my faith goes beyond theology and religion and requires considerable work and effort. My faith demands—this is not optional—my faith demands that I do whatever I can, whenever I can, for as long as I can with whatever I have to try to make a difference.

Jimmy Carter

As quoted in The New York Times Magazine

...he allowed himself to be swayed by his conviction that human beings are not born once and for all on the day their mothers give birth to them, but their life obliges them over and over again to give birth to themselves.

Gabriel García Marquez

Love in the Time of Cholera

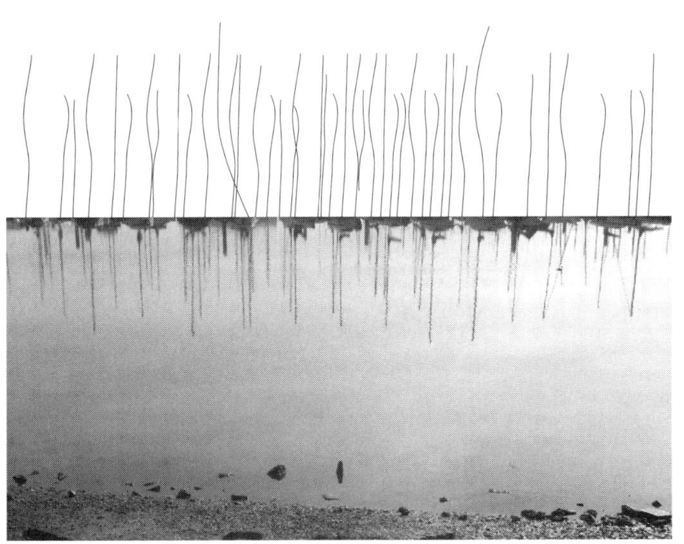

If we knew we were on the right road, having to leave it would mean endless despair. But we are on a road that only leads to a second one and then to a third one and so forth. And the real highway will not be sighted for a long, long time, perhaps never. So we drift in doubt. But also in an unbelievable diversity. Thus the accomplishment of hopes remains an always-expected miracle. But in compensation, the miracle remains forever possible.

Franz Kafka

Diaries

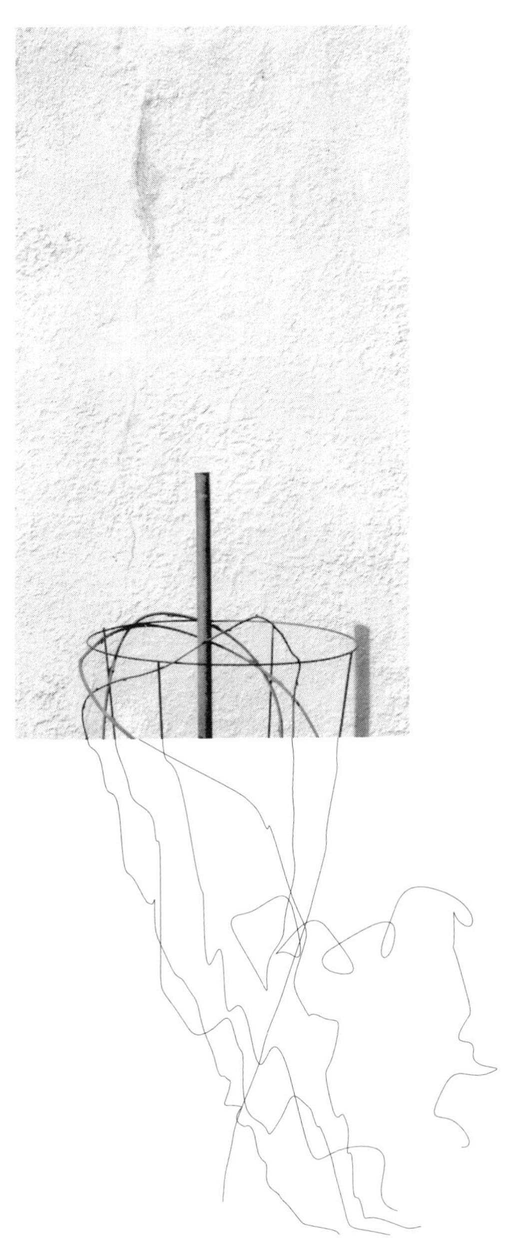

For God to me, it seems

Is a verb

Not a noun,

Proper or improper,

Is the articulation

Not the art...

Is loving, not the abstraction of love...

Yes, God is a verb,

The most active, connoting the vast harmonic

Recording of the universe

From the unleashed chaos of energy.

Bukminster Fuller

Do I contradict myself?

Very well then...I contradict myself;

I am large...I contain multitudes.

Walt Whitman

Songs of Myself

Why has the expression of joy, of spontaneity, even of affection become something that so often seems like a weighty problem which has to be worried about, discussed, with new strategies to be tried out, then those strategies observed and judged, and ourselves with them?

It would be quite wrong to over-idealize childhood, but is impossible not to wonder if it has to be the price of adulthood to feel vulnerable, awkward, tense, locked-in, needy or lonely. To sit chilly and cramped on a hard park bench, perhaps alongside someone you know well, while children, infants and dogs experience their aliveness to the full. **(p. 4)**

Stephanie Dowrick

Intimacy and Solitude

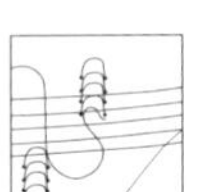

I left the woods for as good a reason as I went there. Perhaps it seemed to me that I had several more lives to live, and could not spare any more time for that one...I learned this, at least, by my experiment; that if one advances confidently in the directions of his dreams, and endeavors to live the life which he has imagined, he will meet with a success unexpected in common hours.

Henry David Thoreau

Walden

near death for a musician— a new life experiencing "the presence"

Trust isn't the kind of thing you exactly learn—you either trust or you don't. And when you feel you can't trust, you can't let go. So why is it sometimes so difficult to trust? I've found that there are often obstacles between us and our capacity to trust, and in order to overcome them, we first need to know what they are and how they work. . . .These three examples indicate three major obstacles to trust: worries about self-image, the feelings that things are out of your control, and doubts and fears about your own ability. **(pps. 78–79)**

Barry Green

The Inner Game of Music

As civilization advances, the sense of wonder declines. Such decline is an alarming symptom of our state of mind. Mankind will not perish for want of information, but only for want of appreciation. The beginning of our happiness lies in the understanding that life without wonder is not worth living. What we lack is not a will to believe, but a will to wonder. **(p. 41)**

The sense for the "miracles which are daily with us," the sense for the "continual marvels," is the source of prayer. There is no worship, no music, no love, if we take for granted the blessings or defeats of living....This is one of the goals of the Jewish way of living: to experience commonplace deeds as spiritual adventures, to feel hidden love and wisdom in all things. **(p. 43)**

The sense of the ineffable, the awareness of the grandeur and mystery of living, is shared by all men, and it is in the depth of such awareness that acts and thoughts of religion are full of meaning. **(p. 48)**

Abraham Joshua Heschel

Between God and Man

Author's Note: I had been in Mississippi to conduct the All-State Honors Choir. I returned home, and I thought it strange that I did not hear from the organizing host, Susanne. Several months later, this e-mail appeared on my screen. Susanne had dropped me off at the airport, and continued on to drop her students off at their homes. The next day, Sunday, at the age of 42, she suffered a stroke. There were no warning signs, and she had no history of problems that would lead to such a condition. She completely recovered and wrote the following to me. We share it with you in the hope that you will value each minute of your life and your time making music, and you continue to invest in love during your life.

I can remember only limited things and events. I was in intensive care for a week. My family would make the trek from the waiting room to see me, unconscious, every few hours. The rest of the time, they slept in the waiting room that entire week. So they have yet another perspective on this: the prospect of losing a family member. Anyway, I was so sleepy in intensive care! I only remember two or three things that entire week. My family coming in once, a visit from one of the school administrators who said comforting words to me, and one of my best friends and her husband.

Then there was the *Presence.* It was like my life was in complete turmoil until this Presence began to walk beside me. We were in a calm place outside...a field. I remember looking down and the grass was green. The atmosphere was muted. There were no golden streets, no tunnels of light for me, no loved ones who had passed before me; just this most peaceful, beautiful, clarifying, yes, I said clarifying feeling: it was that I felt balanced finally, that all unnecessary things fell away. I felt completely accepted, completely loved unconditionally. It was as if my life was a rope knotted and frayed and suddenly it was smooth! I didn't realize I had such distress in my life until I felt this peace, this acceptance. Since that time, I have this incredible perspective. Though I have to fight to keep the peace, for we live in such a noisy world, it is that peace I crave. I still remember the experience and I believe that it changed my life. I will never be the same.

I have learned a lot from the stroke. I find out just about every day new ways that the stroke made me a better person. I guess the most obvious is how I handle adversity. Things just don't bother me like they used to.

I have a new perspective.

- I want to create beautiful music.
- I want to be with my son.
- I want to laugh every day.
- I don't want to hurry and rush around.
- I want to seek peace.
- I want to remember what really matters, those simple things: listening to a giggling son, hearing a beautiful phrase of music, seeing the expression on someone's face in rehearsal, taking time to listen.
- Showing compassion.
- Being kind and forgiving.
- Reading a good book.
- Watching an old movie.
- Putting on music from your high school and college days and dancing around the room with the windows open in the springtime.
- Picking flowers...

Oh let me see, what else? Is this cornball?

But honestly, this is what matters...it really is the little stuff that gives such great poignant pleasure. The difference is that after the stroke, you recognize all of the above. So while you are experiencing it, there is this bittersweet feeling of, "I am so glad I got another chance at life, another time to do this and enjoy it down to my toes!"

Susanne Spencer-VanDyke
Susanne Spencer-VanDyke is Director of Choral Activities at Northwest Mississippi Community College, Senatobia, Mississippi. She also serves as Director of Chancel Choir, Batesville Presbyterian Church, Batesville, Mississippi.

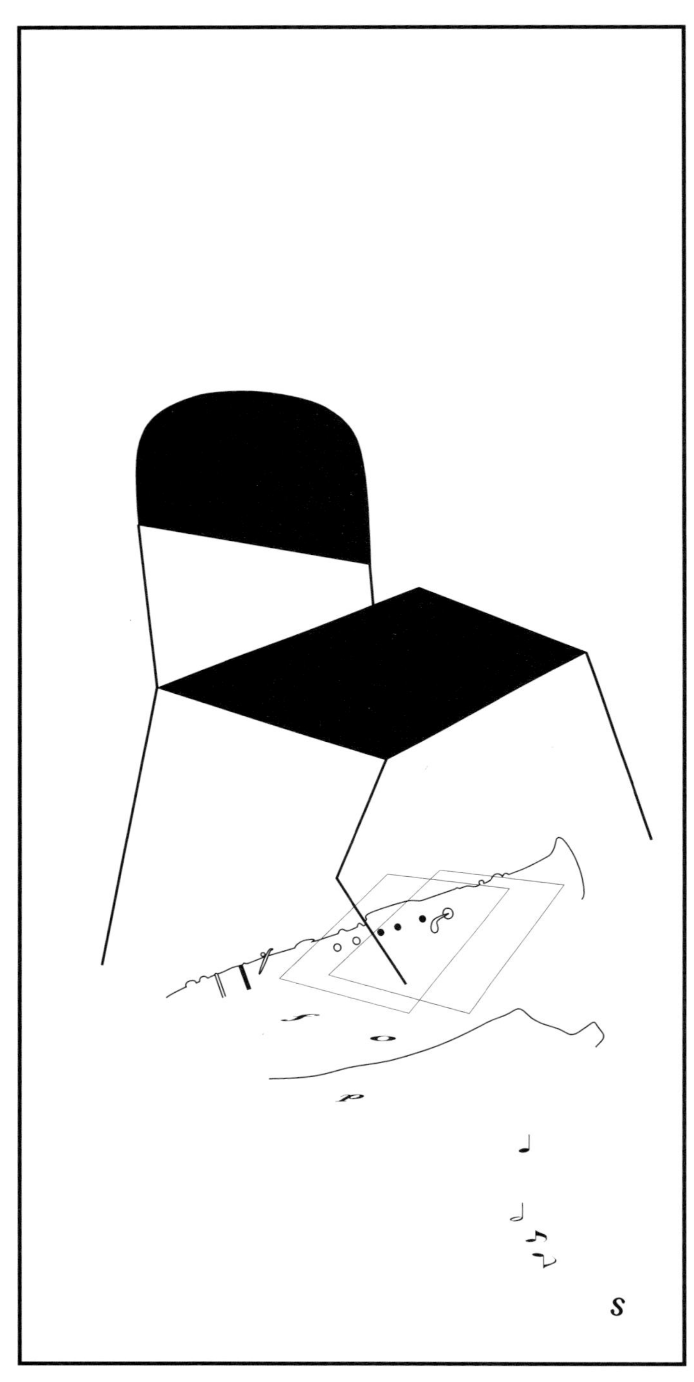

musical child abuse

Author's Note: *I believe that everyone has many stories, such as the one that follows, lurking silently in their past. What many musicians do not realize is that such events cause an inability to either access their own inner musical voices, or perhaps even more serious, deny them the ability to connect with others through their music. Far worse, perhaps, is the fact that they doubt their own musicianship. Gone untended and unacknowledged, these events can profoundly affect one's entire musical life and one's ability to find music within him and within others. Abuses, unfortunately, seem to be part of the life process. Many persons refuse to acknowledge their role in the music-making process. Yet, if one really listens to their music, one can hear those abuses come through the music. For example, lines that do not sing, hard, metallic sounds, a predominance of dark sounds, and energetic rhythmic sounds that are encased in anger. The rhythm of such musicians tends to be violent at times. Colors and textures are either limited in their music-making palates or consist of a relatively narrow spectrum of musical color. By revisiting these profound musical events in one's life, one can acknowledge that they have happened, place them in their proper perspective, and perhaps, see their musical selves in a fresh light and move toward both new human and musical potentials.*

I was so excited. I came home from the fourth grade musical instruments demonstration night with a new clarinet! I went up to my bedroom, and carefully opened the new black lined case. I admired the velvet interior, the shiny keys; all stuff of fascination for any fourth grader. I was a bit daunted, however, by all the metal keys on the clarinet. It seemed improbable that such a complicated series of springs, keys, and levers could produce such a beautiful sound. My first lesson was in two days; I could hardly wait.

The appointed day and hour arrived. Music lessons were taught in the boiler room of my elementary school. It didn't matter. I was so excited for my first lesson.

I arrived, and Mr. G (as he was called) sat in a chair. He was nattily dressed and had a sharp crew cut. I can remember his shoes, too. Military issue, patent leather and *thick* rubber soles. As I peered in the boiler room door, I heard a voice saying "James." I said "Yes," and slithered into the room. Mr. G. sat in a metal folding chair. I noticed two things immediately. The battered drumstick which he seemed to cling to like a ceremonial mace, and the severely dented left leg of the metal folding chair.

He guided me through the process of assembling the instrument, attaching the reed, and making my first sound. I was so excited. We then opened the lesson book. I learned my first few fingerings: F, open G in addition to counting whole notes, half notes, whole rests, and half rests. Mr. G explained how to "count." He explained, "You move your foot up an down while you play. The whole note gets four beats. Listen."

He began to sing the exercise I was about to play. But one strange thing, I thought. As he sang, he kept "the beat" not by tapping his foot as he instructed me to do, but by hitting the chair of music stand with a drumstick *very loudly.* I remember thinking it was very annoying, but tried not to pay attention to it. So, I went home to practice.

I returned the next week with my lesson learned well. He told me I was a "natural" and that I was already producing a beautiful tone. (I think my Mom would disagree). I was excited to share something with him. I told him that I

Musician's Spirit

learned the lesson very quickly, but wanted to do more practice. So, I told him how I became curious about all the funny keys on the clarinet. *And then I told him of my discovery.* I told him that I had "figured out" that I could play the "tune" of my lesson starting on any one of the keys of the clarinet (little did I know that I had taught myself to transpose!) I asked, "Want to hear what I have done?"

As I looked at him, I could see how angry he was. A huge vein popped out of his neck. I started to play anyway. He took the drumstick and hit me across the fingers of my right hand. "Never, *never* do anything that I do not tell you to do!" My fingers throbbed and were black and blue. I was also sobbing uncontrollably. "I have done a terrible thing...I have disobeyed the teacher." I immediately became afraid that my parents would likewise be angry. I packed up the instrument and went back to class.

The next lesson involved learning 3/4 and 6/8 time. The book said, "Three beats in a measure and a quarter note gets a beat, but sometimes this is felt in one." Then, when you turn the page, the next page contained the same tunes, only notated in 6/8. The book said that there were six beats in the bar, and that the eighth note got the beat. Yet, as I sat in my bedroom and practiced, both the 3/4 exercises and the 6/8 exercises sounded the same to me, although they looked different. Surely, I thought, I must have misunderstood. Never fear, I thought. Mr. G. will explain it.

So, having recovered from my drumstick pummeling, I arrived at my lesson. I wanted to ask him this question. He said, "No questions, James, just play." I played my lesson perfectly. He told me it was excellent. I then interrupted and asked, "But Mr. G, how come these two pages sound the same, but *look* different?" Before I knew it, he took out the drumstick, and beat me over the knuckles again. I was terrified.

What had I done that was so wrong? It was confusing, 3/4 and 6/8 sounded the same and looked different.

When I arrived home after school, my Mom noticed my hands. "What happened?" she asked. "Oh, I caught them in a door at school," I told her. "Must have been a pretty hard slam," my mom said. I said, "Yeah," and went to my room.

Let it be known that I cried every day for a few weeks over this. I faked being sick for my lesson the next week, and then went to the nurse's office the following week. Anything to avoid Mr. G. I also began to believe that I was the problem here. I reasoned that my question was stupid, and I was not meant to be a musician.

Playing the clarinet became a burden. It seemed every time I picked it up I was "scared." I did everything to avoid lessons, although I would play for hours in my room. Lessons with Mr. G seemed to be on a downward spiral after that. At one point in one lesson, I was sweating and shaking so badly he just blurted out, "You really have no talent at this, why do you continue? You are wasting *my* time."

Now I really felt great! I had no idea why I continued with those hideous lessons. Well, I guess the reason was because I loved music and was hardheaded enough to continue despite my fear. That fear of the instrument continued through my undergraduate and graduate programs. In the back of my mind those words of his always haunted me. It also seemed that every time I picked up the clarinet, I was scared of something.

Until a number of years later (32 to be exact), I was forced to revisit these lessons. I realized that much of my spiritual closure as a musician was due, almost without exception, to the physical and verbal abuse I received from this very unhappy human being. When I relived the events, told myself the story again, it seemed to free me. My music making approached new levels.

I do not understand why Mr. G taught me that way. I also have forgiven him a long time ago. He lives near my mother. Every time I have a concert or publish a new book, I walk to his home and put a program or book in his mailbox. We have not spoken for some 25 years. I doubt that he understands the *real* reason why I leave him the books and the programs. And, I fear that many more children never will know the joy of music because of the abuse they suffered with him.

I now love the clarinet again.

V
being a fool

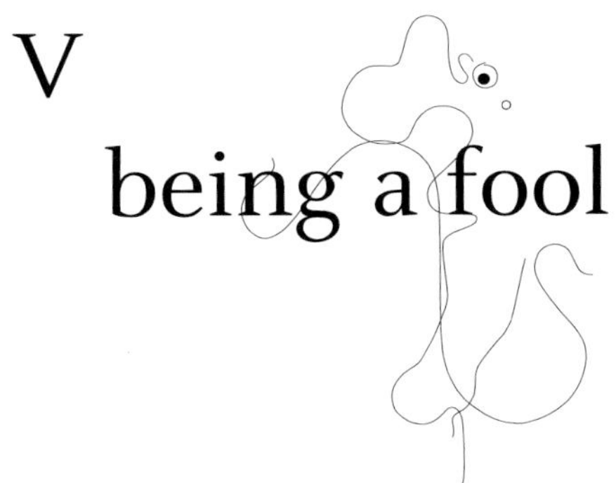

If there is one thing I know about, it's being a fool. During the years of performing on the streets, people would often ask me, 'What are you? Are you a mime or you a clown?' I would always answer, 'No, I am a fool.'

Now before you start analyzing this too deeply, I never said I was an idiot. I am a fool and as such, part of an age-old tradition. Modern day entertainment has become overwhelmed with comedians and boobs that resort to foolishness to get a laugh. But true fools are something our contemporary culture often lacks.

Fools fill a function. A fool can take the world and turn it inside out and show you something that's new. A good fool can make fun of everything and everyone and teach us not to take ourselves too seriously.

Your inner fool permits you to be perfectly imperfect. Your personal fool gives you a ticket for a free ride in that fun house hidden inside you. Your fun house has some scary dark corners? The fool casts light on those corners and makes you laugh. Just when you think life is really serious and grown up, the fool will get you. The fool is all about laughing at yourself.

The fool is about transformation. It's who you become after you stop taking yourself so seriously. We all have that dark delicious place—the forbidden zone. What's yours? Being a fool means you accept who you are, fun house and all. **(pps. 145-149).**

Robert Shields

Cats, fish and Fools

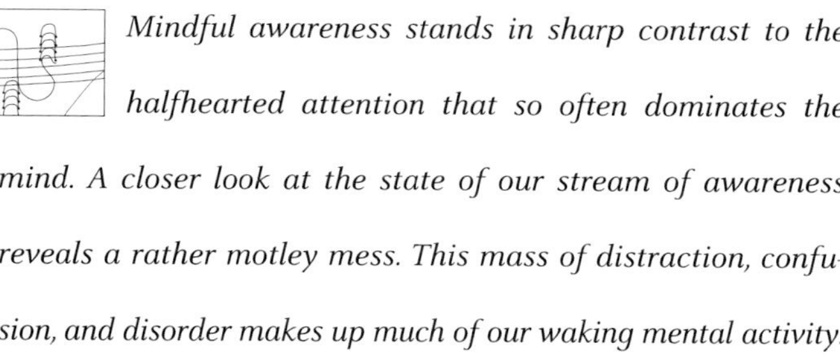

Mindful awareness stands in sharp contrast to the halfhearted attention that so often dominates the mind. A closer look at the state of our stream of awareness reveals a rather motley mess. This mass of distraction, confusion, and disorder makes up much of our waking mental activity.

The antidote to this distractedness is mindfulness. While ordinary attention swings rather wildly from focus to focus, carried here and there by distractions—random thoughts, fleeting memories, captivating fantasies, snatches of things seen, heard, or otherwise sensed—by contrast, mindfulness is distraction resistant. A sustained attention, mindfulness keeps its beam of focus fully in the moment, and maintains that focus on to the next moment, then the next and the next—and so on. If distractedness breeds emotional turmoil, the ability to sustain our gaze, to keep looking, is one essential quality of awareness in working with our emotions. **(p. 30)**

Staying in a mindful state requires that we let go of any and all thoughts as they come and go. This includes our most troubling thoughts: instead of getting caught up in them and swept away, and so feeding the feelings of distress that go with them, we let go of those thoughts—and the feelings that go with them. **(p. 33)**

When we are mindful—free of preconception and judgment—we are automatically imbued with light-heartedness. We can step far enough back from ourselves to make room for a sense of humor and playfulness. **(p. 42)**

Tara Bennett-Goleman

Emotional Alchemy

Awe is an intuition for the dignity of all things, a realization that things not only are what they are but also stand, however remotely, for something supreme. Awe is a sense for the transcendence, for the reference everywhere to the mystery beyond all things. It enables us to perceive in the world intimations of the divine...to sense the ultimate in the common and the simple; to feel in the rush of the passing stillness of the eternal. **(p. 9)**

Abraham Joshua Heschel

I Asked for Wonder

The first step in this clear seeing comes when we pause and become mindful, interrupting the flow of our habitual thoughts, feelings, and reactions. **(p. 43)**

If you stay mindful as thoughts appear in your awareness, they reveal their empty nature and eventually dissolve. Let them vanish on their own, without adding to them in any way. If you become too involved with thinking the thoughts, you can reconnect with the sensation of breathing at any point. **(p. 47)**

When we can recognize an emotion clearly and openly, our relationship to it changes. We no longer have to resist it to cling to it. We can learn to accept it with a clear non-reactive awareness. **(p. 48)**

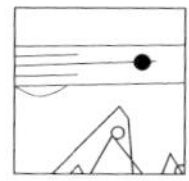

If you are not sure where your attention should be at any point, you can return to breathing. **(p. 48)**

Tara-Bennett-Goleman

Emotional Alchemy

george

Music has not failed us; it is we at times that have failed music. We have depended upon gadgets and gimmicks, methods and procedures—many of which are outdated—to make our music successful. And all the while our principal purpose should be that of allowing the music to speak for itself. **(p. 84)**

When a mutual and sympathetic understanding of the human spirit is built, people finally become persons. **(p. 149)**

Howard Swan

Conscience of a Profession

*Remember that there is meaning beyond absurdity. Know that every deed counts, that every word is power....Above all, remember that you must build your life as if it were a work of art....***(p. ix)**

Abraham Joshua Heschel

I Asked for Wonder

James Jordan

Let me say from the onset that this story could be about any student, any teacher. Unfortunately, it is my story. I pray that it hasn't happened to you. If it hasn't, count your blessings and love the people you teach and make music with. If it has, you will understand of what I write.

George Miller brightened every room he walked into. I first knew of George because he lived across the street from me. I knew his father well because he was a professor in a local university and was also an accomplished musician. When George had entered the ninth grade, he was not involved in any musical activities. His father tried to convince him to join the high school choir that I conducted. George, like most ninth grade boys, resisted the push. His father came over to the house and asked what could I do to get George to sing. I offered to talk to him.

Our conversation was short and to the point. I basically negotiated a deal. I said that if he would join the choir, I would allow him to leave at any time, and support the decision with his father. George thought that this was a win situation for him. I knew that after meeting him that it was a win situation for the choir.

George showed up for the first rehearsal. I had auditioned him, and placed him in the tenor section; he was a wonderful young tenor. The first rehearsal, we read through one of the Mendelssohn *Sechs Spruche,* Op 79. I *knew* from his eyes that George would not be leaving. After rehearsal, he was bubbling over. What amazed me is that he was unabashed in his excitement for the music and for the singing! Over the years, I grew to admire this young man not only as a musician, but also as a human being.

George was the ideal choir member. He *never* missed rehearsal. He was always prepared, and he always learned his music. In the tenth and eleventh grade, he enrolled in every music course the school offered. George also became a good friend, stopping by the house frequently to see if there was anything that he could do to help out. I did ask him to check in on my wife when I was away, which he did dutifully.

On one of his frequent visits, he arrived on a little moped. He loved the thing. I mentioned to him that if he was going to ride that, he really should wear a helmet. He remarked that he never went fast, and didn't actually ride the thing that much.

Several weeks later, I arrived at school. An entourage of students met me at school. "Did you hear what happened to George last night?" I had not heard. "He was hit by a tractor-trailer on Route 15. He is in the hospital in intensive care on life support."

My heart sank. I left school immediately and headed to the hospital. I thought to myself...I really don't want to see him in this condition, but I need to be there for his parents. I arrived at the hospital and went directly to intensive care, and took a seat in the waiting room. Almost immediately, his father John appeared. "Oh, Jim, I am so glad you are here. George will be overjoyed you came."

With those words, I breathed a sigh of relief. I thought, "He must be improving." But with that thought, his father said, "Things look very bad. He is brain dead, and we have some decisions to make today. Come in and see Georgie." My heart almost stopped. I did not want to go in. I wanted to remember him as he was. "Be prepared, Jim, he doesn't look anything like Georgie." With that, his father took my sweaty hand and guided me into the room.

There he lay. Tubes and machines seemingly connected everywhere. Severe swelling and bruising made him look nothing like him, which actually made it easier for me. We came to the side of the bed and I instinctively grabbed his hand and started to cry quietly. The hand was lifeless, but still I held it. His father whispered in his ear, "Jim Jordan is here."

Immediately, the lifeless hand gripped mine. I knew he knew I was there. He kept releasing his grip and grabbed over and over again. As this was happening, a very strange thing happened to me. Instead of being in that hospital room, I had literally hundreds of flashbacks of George in a rehearsal, George in a lesson, George in a concert, George laughing. All of the flashbacks had sound. It seemed that every musical moment I shared with this singer was imbedded in my psyche. The flashbacks ended. I leaned over and whispered in his ear that I loved him, and left.

George died that evening. The high school choir sang for the funeral. We were all deeply touched by this loss. But for me, it was a seminal point in my teaching. At the funeral, his mother and father shared with me that singing in the choir was his life. Singing changed him. They related to me how fondly he spoke of his singing and how he loved it so.

I spent much time thinking about all of this and arrived at a stark, but true fact. I had no idea that what I did had such a profound influence on this young man. Nor was I aware that it is a necessity that I give the most of myself each day in rehearsal to every student. I thought about how much guilt I would have now if I didn't feel I had given this student my all. I also began to realize how deeply this student, unbeknownst to me, had touched *me.*

There is not a day that goes by that I do not think of this young man. To this day, a photograph taken in school of a theory class for a local paper with he and I in the picture hangs in my office. Whenever I begin to walk into a rehearsal and feel that I am not fully alive, I think of George. I think that I cannot allow the ensuing rehearsal to become a missed opportunity.

Through the years, the memory of George has served me well. He is with me every day. I really believe he sits on my shoulder and is my guardian angel.

Am I right, George?

Author's Note:

This essay is dedicated to the memory of George A. Miller

Awareness of God does not come by degrees from timidity to intellectual temerity; it is not a decision reached at the crossroads of doubt. It comes when, drifting in the wilderness, having gone astray, we suddenly behold the immutable polar star, out of endless anxiety, out of denial of despair, we should burst out in speechless crying. **(p. 7)**

Abraham Joshua Heschel

I Asked for Wonder

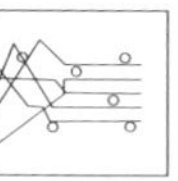

Stillness is our most intense mode of action. It is our moments of deep quiet that is born every idea, emotion, and drive, which we eventually honor with the name of action. Our most emotionally active life is lived in our dreams, and our cells renew themselves most industriously in sleep. We reach highest in meditation, and farthest in prayer. In stillness, every human being is great; he is free from the experience of hostility; he is a poet, and most like an angel. **(p. 330)**

Leonard Bernstein

Findings

HELP SAVE

love thyself—first

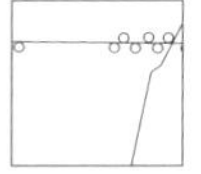

One cannot know thee until you know thee.

St. Augustine

It takes three things to attain a sense of significant being: **God, A Soul, and a Moment.** *And the three are always here.* **(p. 65)**

A human being has not only a body but also a face. A face cannot be grafted or interchanged. A face is a message, a face speaks, often unbeknown to the person. Is not the human face a living mixture of mystery and meaning? We are all able to see it, and are all able to describe it. Is it not a strange marvel that among so many hundreds of millions of faces, no two faces are alike? And that no face remains quite the same for more than an instant? The most exposed part of the body, it is the least describable, a synonym for an incarnation of uniqueness. Can we look at a face as if it were a commonplace? **(p. 48)**

Looking upon myself from the perspective of society, I am an average person. Facing myself intimately, I regard myself as unique, as exceedingly precious, not to be exchanged for anything else.

No one will live my life for me; no one will think my thoughts for me or dream my dreams.

In the eyes of the world, I am an average man. But to my heart I am not an average man. To my heart I am of great moment. The challenge I face is how to actualize the quiet eminence of my being. **(p. 47)**

Abraham Joshua Heschel

I Asked for Wonder

In the summer of 2000, I had a startling revelation that came about quite by accident. While I had thought about the subject many times, I had never really verbalized it, until this day in July.

I was rehearsing the Stravinsky *Symphony of Psalms* with the Westminster High School Vocal Institute. This institute had been in place for some fifty years. This summer, I decided I would tackle the *Symphony of Psalms.* I felt certain that between myself and a very talented conducting staff, we could teach the piece. But I was very worried about how I could get these very young students to travel to the spiritual places necessary in order to do Stravinsky's voice justice.

Things were actually going very well. After the notes of the first movement were learned, we discussed in detail how the concept of entrapment was the theme of the first movement. I was amazed at how quickly these young students latched onto the concept! Instead of examining why this "entrapment" was so easy for them to access, I just proceeded with the piece.

We then set out to learn the second movement. The difficult double fugue proved to be a challenge indeed. In order to give some shape to that movement, we sang the entire movement the best we could in order to reach the incredible transition into the third movement, with the text of "Alleluia."

When we arrived there, the choir sang all the right notes and had the proper rhythm concepts in place. The music at this point *should* have sung, but it didn't. To my ears, the pitches and rhythm were all correct, but the sound was hollow, almost vapid. I stopped the choir and wanted to share some type of story. Out of my mouth came the following statement: "If you want to sing something beautifully, you must first believe that **you** are beautiful."

All of a sudden, there was a deafening silence in the room. I knew I had hit some kind of communal nerve. All eyes were on me. I repeated the phrase. The room remained deafeningly quiet. As I looked around the room, I saw these students as I had never seen them before—incredibly vulnerable. Many flashing thoughts went through my mind. I talked with them about the importance of self-love not only for a musician, but its role in life in general. After that, we sang the Alleluia passage again; it was unbelievably beautiful.

The rehearsal ended. I was turned away from the rehearsal room packing my briefcase when I turned around to respond to someone's question. About 60 students were waiting to talk to me! Before I left to eat dinner, I spoke with each student. Tears were the order of the hour. All thanked me for what I said. Many had a remark that frightened me: "I never thought of myself as a beautiful person." The tears around me validated my suspicions. These students were growing up in a world that was making incredible demands upon them. The fashion conscious, body conscious eras we are living through have contributed to this terrible self-image syndrome. Many students confided in me that they had or were considering taking their lives. Depression and worthlessness pervaded their eyes.

I lay awake most of that night. I thought of all of those who talked to me, and worried about the many who did not speak to me. I knew that many of them were as restless that night as I was.

The next day in rehearsal, I storied. I talked of how we all must look inside and search for what is beautiful in each one of us. I talked about how the world encourages us *not* to know and love ourselves in so many ways. We talked of the simplistic relationship between beauty of inner self and how music reflects how we love ourselves. We talked about how we must love ourselves in order for there to be love in the sound. What is the sound of love in a choral sound?

They then sang. It was incredible. Impeccably in tune; brilliant in color; musical line that moved forward with a direction and arch. Clarity of rhythm. Perfect balance, almost transparent sound. I thought to myself, this is an *honest* sound! When we stopped, there was a quiet that descended onto the room, but it was different from the day before. This quiet was filled with joy and love; the energy in room told you that. It was clear that they all had thought about this; I was also convinced that the role of the "story" allowed them to connect with themselves as they had never connected before. On this day, I was convinced of how difficult it is to be an artist in these times, and how much these students had to deal with growing up in this complicated world. They needed to connect with themselves in order to sing this (or any) music.

Love of Self is the only way to that connection.

We need to teach more about loving ourselves, because after all, isn't music about love and beauty in sound?

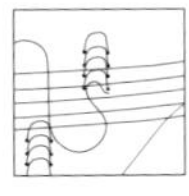

Each night when I go to sleep, I die. And the next morning, when I wake up, I am reborn.

Mahatma Gandhi

James Jordan

Forcing yourself to use restricted means is the sort of restraint that liberates invention. It obliges you to make a kind of progress that you can't even imagine in advance. **(p. 55)**

Painting is stronger than I am. It makes me do what it wants. **(p. 70)**

What's the use of disguises in a work of art? What counts is what is spontaneous, impulsive. That is the truthful truth. What we impose upon ourselves does not emanate from ourselves. **(p. 85)**

Pablo Picasso

In His Words

How then may we do this, if we want to? What must we do to let our light shine, we ordinary people? Well, in the first place, it is not what we do but who we are that counts; it is not in doing but in being and that is a hard lesson for such achievement-oriented souls as we. Phillips Brooks reminded us that preaching is 'truth through personality,' and that means that what a person is speaks so loudly that we cannot hear what the person says. 'Being" comes from within; the light shines out, not in. **(p. 118)**

Peter Gomes

Sermons

I am done with great things and big things, great institutions and big success; and am for those tiny, invisible molecular moral forces that work from individual to individual through the crannies of the world, like so many rootlets, or like the capillary oozing of water, yet which, if you give them time, will rend the hardest moments of man's pride. **(p. 119)**

William James

Sermons by Peter Gomes

all you need is love

The day will come when after we have mastered the winds, the waves, the tides and gravity, we shall harness for God the energies of love. Then, for the second time in the history of the world, mankind will have discovered fire. **(p. 186)**

Pierre Teilhard De Chardin

Quantum Theology

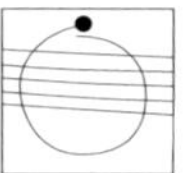

"Mitch, you asked about caring for people you don't even know. But can I tell you the thing I'm learning with this disease?"

"What's that?"

"The most important thing in life is to learn how to give out love, and to let it come in."

His voice dropped to a whisper. "Let it come in. We think we don't deserve love; we think if we let it in we'll become too soft. But a wise man named Levine said it right. He said, 'Love is the only rational act'."

He repeated it carefully, pausing for effect. "Love is the only rational act." **(p. 52)**

Mitch Albom

Tuesdays with Morrie

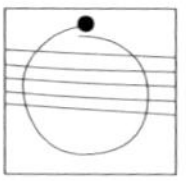

Where there is great love, there are always miracles.

Willa Cather

The Artist's Way at Work by Mark Bryan

Musician's Spirit

If I have all the eloquence of men or of angels, but speak without love, I am simply a gong booming or a cymbal clashing. If I have the gift of prophecy, understanding all the mysteries there are, and knowing everything, and if I have faith in all its fullness, to move mountains, but without love, I am nothing at all.

Love is always patient and kind; it is never jealous; love is never boastful or conceited; it is never rude or selfish; it does not take offense, and is not resentful. Love takes no pleasure in other people's sins but delights in the truth; it is always ready to excuse, to trust, to hope, and to endure whatever comes.

Love does not come to an end. But if there are gifts of prophecy, the time will come when they must fail; or the gift of languages; it will not continue forever; and knowledge—for this, too, the time will come when it must fail. For our knowledge is imperfect and our prophesying is imperfect; but once perfection comes, all imperfect things disappear. When I was a child, I used to talk like a child, and think like a child, and argue like a child, but now I am a man, all childish ways are put behind me. Now we are seeing a dim reflection in a mirror; but we shall be seeing face to face. The knowledge that I have now is imperfect; but then I shall know as fully as I am known.

In short, there are three things that last: faith, hope and love; and the greatest of these is love.

1 Corinthians 13

It was an incredibly stressful day. Elizabeth, my daughter, had just been diagnosed with Juvenile Diabetes at Children's Hospital in Philadelphia. All day, I studied and learned a new protocol for dealing with this condition in Elizabeth; blood testing, insulin injections, and carbohydrate counting were now a vital part of all our lives.

Elizabeth asked Daddy to stay with her that night in the hospital. The rooms at Children's Hospital are equipped with adult sleeper beds right alongside the child's bed. So, when evening came, I set up the bed and went to sleep.

It was difficult to fall asleep. Elizabeth was in a semi-private room with two other children. Across from Elizabeth was a young girl hospitalized for asthma. She was fast asleep. But through the drawn curtain divider, a baby cried, almost wailed, endlessly. Frustrated, I kept hitting the nurse call button. I must have rung that bell no less than ten times in an hour, with no response. My frustration grew with every push of the button.

Finally, I leapt out of the bed to see what the problem was through the curtain. When I looked into the next bed, there lay an infant who had more tubes connected to her than I could imagine. Her cleft palate was very prominent, and she seemed to have some type of skin condition. She also had one arm that was congenitally malformed. It was, in many ways, both horrific and surreal. This child wailed and wailed. When I looked in she looked at me and seemed to wail even louder.

Parental instinct, I suppose, kicked in. I bounded to the bed and just picked up this child. The crying stopped immediately. She looked at me and smiled.

It dawned on me what the crying was about. It had nothing to do with her *physical* condition, but her spiritual condition. She needed what every human being needs, to be held and to be loved. I carefully moved over to a rocker near her bed and rocked her for the better part of an hour. As she drifted to sleep in my arms, a nurse appeared.

The nurse apologized for not getting there sooner, but thanked me for the rocker time with the child. I asked about the child. The nurse said she cries endlessly throughout the day. She suspected that it was because the mother had *never* come to the hospital. In fact, no one came to see this child. The mother brought the child to the emergency room, then promptly left.

What this child needed most, perhaps more than the excellent medical attention she was receiving, was *love.* As in *Tuesdays with Morrie,* Morrie told Mitch Albom as he looked back at his life and lay dying, that, "Love is the only rational act."

For musicians, beautiful sounds can only be created from a loving place that loves both self and others. There will be no exquisite intonation, no beautiful line, without an ability to love. That little child in Children's Hospital radiantly illustrated the power of simple love being used to heal and calm. When I conduct choirs, I often think of how wonderful it felt to hold that beautiful, ill child in my arms. It gives me easy access to a loving place. Her eyes gave me love back, and that is the only payment I needed. Her openness, vulnerability, and helplessness brought tears to my eyes.

Did I finally get to bed? No. I stayed up all night rocking that child and watched the sun come up over Philadelphia. Few times in my life have I felt that I had made a difference. I believe I made a difference that day. I have no idea what happened to her. I wish her Godspeed. Elizabeth left the hospital three days later. My job was to visit Elizabeth and that little girl for those several days. My life was enriched through knowing her and holding her.

Silence is neither mute nor talkative...in such silence holy desires, peace and calm of heart, and true purity grow and multiply, in the absence of windy and vain talkativeness...which sows discord. **(p. 77)**

Peter of Celle from The School of Clositer

Monastic Wisdom by Hugh Feiss

the fantasy of flight

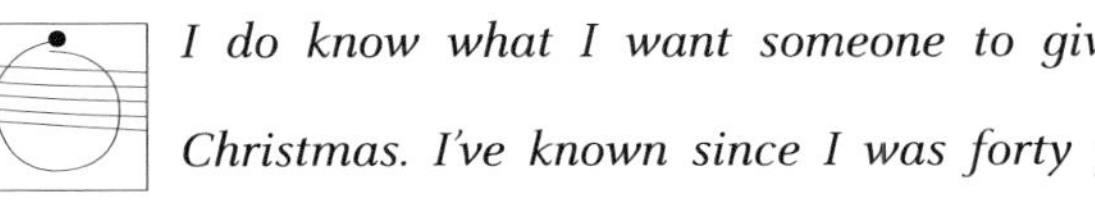

I do know what I want someone to give me for Christmas. I've known since I was forty years old. Wind-up mechanical toys that make noises and go round and round and do funny things. No batteries. Toys that need me to help them out from time to time. The old fashioned painted tin ones I had as a child. That's what I want. Nobody believes me. It's what I want, I tell you. Well, okay, that's close, but not exactly it. It's delight and simplicity that I want. Foolishness and fantasy and noise. Angels and miracles and wonder and innocence and magic. That's closer to what I want.

It's harder to talk about, but what I really, really, really want for Christmas is just this:

I want to be five years old again for an hour.

I want to laugh a lot and cry a lot.

I want to be picked up and rocked to sleep in someone's arms, and carried up to bed just one more time.

I know what I really want for Christmas.

I want my childhood back.

Nobody is going to give me that. I might give at least the memory of it to myself if I try. I know it doesn't make sense, but since when is Christmas about sense, anyway? It is about a child, of long ago and far away, and it is about the child of now. In you and me. Waiting behind the door of our hearts for something wonderful to happen. A child is impractical, unrealistic, simpleminded, and terribly vulnerable to joy. A child who does not need or want to understand gifts of socks or potholders. **(pps. 95–96)**

Robert Fulghum

All I Really Need to Know I Learned in Kindergarten

Well, and what is freedom? First of all, freedom seems to mean the absence of external restraint, the freedom to play. When we are free from external tyrannies, we seek freedom from our inner limitations. We find that in order to play we must be nimble and flexible and imaginative, we must be able to have fun, we must feel enjoyment, and sometimes long imprisonment has made us numb and sluggish. And then we find out that there are, paradoxically, disciplines, which create in us capacities, which allow us to seek our freedom. We learn how to rid ourselves of boredom, of stiffness, our repressed anger, and our anxiety. We become brighter, more energy flows through us, our limbs rise, our spirit comes alive in our tissues. **(p. 22)**

Mary Caroline Richards

Centering

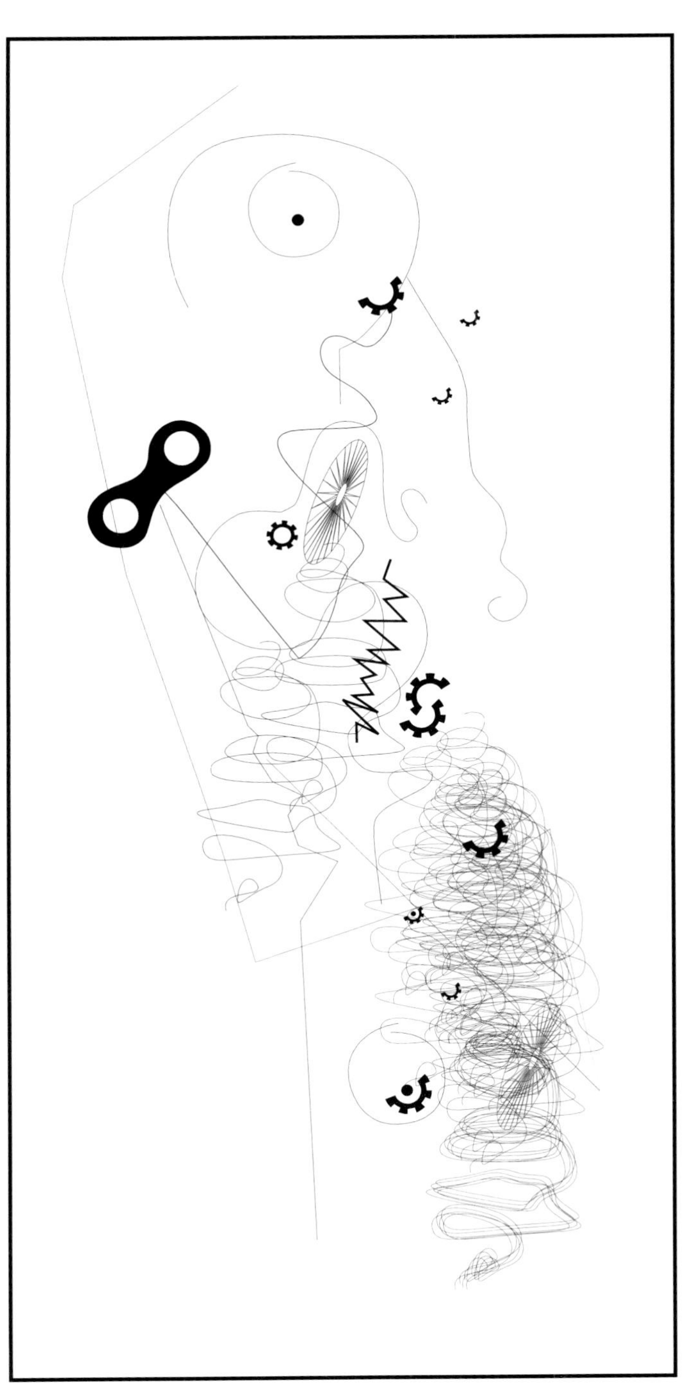

Children paint everyday and love to show their works on walls and refrigerator doors. But as we become adults, we abandon this important soul task of childhood. We assume, I suppose, that children are just learning motor coordination and alphabets. But maybe they are doing something more fundamental: finding forms that reflect what is going on in their souls. **(p. 302)**

Care of the soul is not a project of self-improvement nor a way of being released from the troubles and pains of human existence. It is not at all concerned with living properly or with emotional health. These are the concerns of temporal, heroic, Promethean life. Care of the soul touches another dimension, in no way separate from life, but not identical either with the problem solving that occupies so much of our consciousness. We care for the soul solely by honoring its expressions, by giving it time and opportunity to reveal itself, and by living life in a way that fosters depth, interiority, and quality in which it flourishes. Soul has its own purpose and end. To the soul, memory is more important than planning, art more compelling than reason, and love more fulfilling than understanding. We know we are well on the way toward soul when we feel attachment to the world and the people around us and when we live as much from the heart as from the head.

We know soul is being cared for when our pleasures feel deeper than usual, when we can let go of the need to be free of complexity and confusion, and when compassion takes the place of distrust and fear. **(p. 304)**

Thomas Moore

Care of the Soul

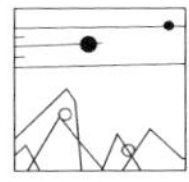

Play is the exultation of the possible. **(p. 198)**

Martin Buber

The Artist's Way by Julia Cameron

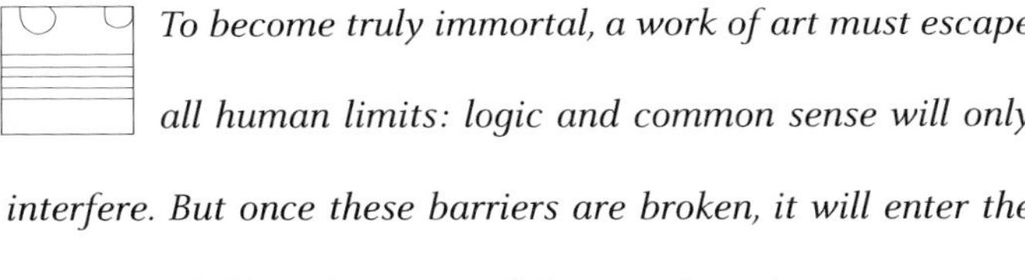

To become truly immortal, a work of art must escape all human limits: logic and common sense will only interfere. But once these barriers are broken, it will enter the realms of childhood vision and dreams. **(p. 84)**

Giorgio De Chirico

The Artist's Way by Julia Cameron

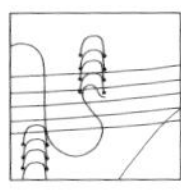

Every artist copes with reality by means of his fantasy. Fantasy, better known as imagination, is his greatest

treasure, his basic equipment for life. And since his work is his life, his fantasy is constantly in play. He dreams life. Psychologists tell us that a child's imagination reaches its peak at the age of six or seven, then is gradually inhibited, diminished to conform with the attitudes of his elders—that is, reality. Alas. Perhaps what distinguishes artists from regular folks is that for whatever reasons, their imaginative drive is less inhibited; they have retained in adulthood more of that five-year-old's fantasy than others have. This is not to say that an artist is the childlike madman the old romantic traditions have made him out to be; he is usually capable of brushing his teeth, keeping track of his love life, or counting his change in a taxicab. When I speak of his **fantasy** *I am not suggesting a constant state of abstraction, but rather the continuous imaginative powers that inform his creative acts as well as his reactions to the world around him. And out of that creativity, and those imaginative reactions come not idle dreams, but truths—all those abiding truth-formations and constellations that nourish us, from Dante to Joyce, from Bach to the Beatles, from Praxiteles to Picasso.* **(pps. 358–359)**

Leonard Bernstein

Findings

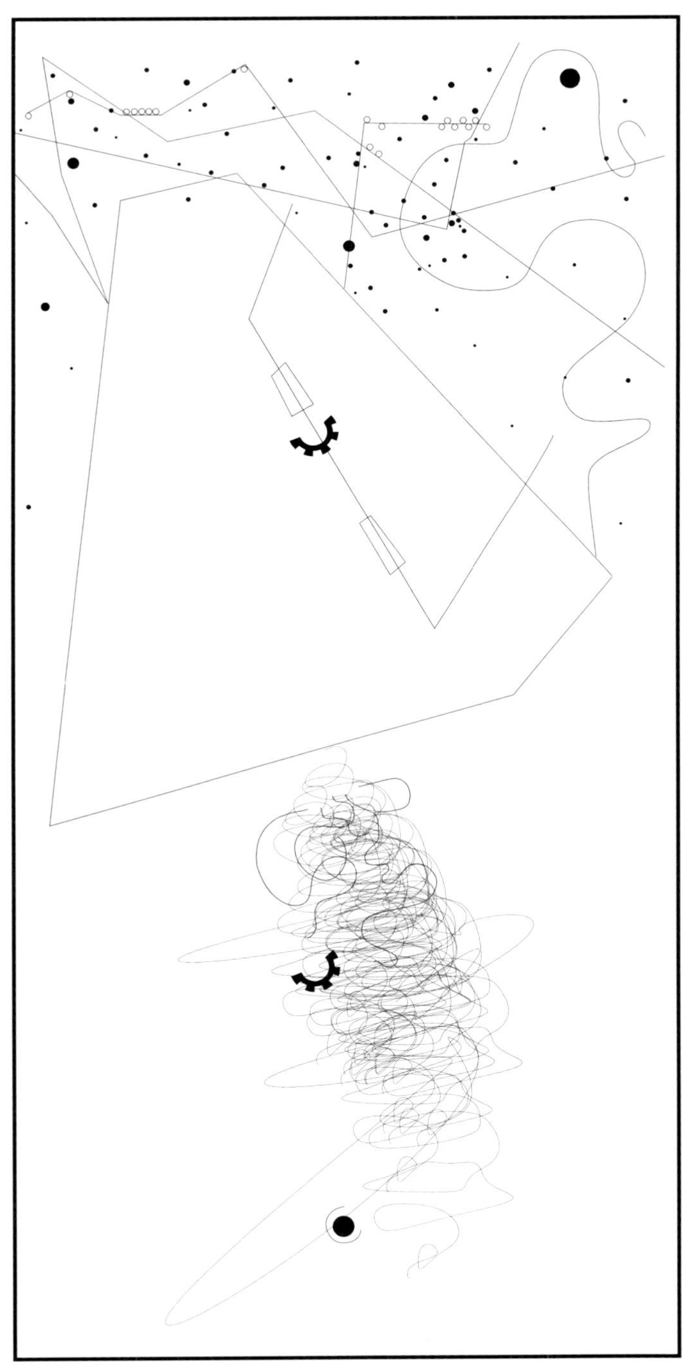

When we are mindful—free of preconception and judgment—we are automatically imbued with a lightheartedness. We can step far enough back from ourselves to make room for a sense of humor and playfulness. **(p. 42)**

Tara Bennett-Goleman

Emotional Alchemy

I have known Don since I was three years old. His grandparents and great-grandparents lived next door to my home. Don lived about a block away, so he would spend his days at Nana's house, come next door, and play with me.

For the most part, we spent much of our waking lives with each other until the age of13, and a substantial portion together until we were 18. Although we have never talked about it, he was and is my best friend; a soul mate of sorts. We shared much in growing up, most of it in what had to be the happiest times of our lives. I can't remember us ever fighting about anything. Don was the right kind of soul friend for me. He was my opposite in temperament. He was always calm, patient, and quiet. I learned much from him growing up.

We also had fun doing crazy things. The things weren't insanely crazy; they were just out of the normal—fantasy play. Don reminded me of the one incident I had forgotten about in a recent e-mail. He said, "Do you remember the rocket ship?"

I had totally forgotten about this major event in my life. *Yes. The Rocket Ship!* I smiled broadly and went back to that time. We must have been in either first or second grade. Alan Shepard had just orbited the earth; there was talk of landing a man on the moon! (Imagine that!)

Donny and I were always building things. When we did, my mom always yelled at me because I seemed to always step on every rusty nail in a one-mile radius. I'd had more tetanus shots than any human being deserves in a lifetime (my mom was a nurse—need I say more?) So on this occasion, we decided that we'd build our own spaceship.

We cleared an area in my basement by the water heater (water was located there so it could supply the spaceship). We built it out of a fire-retardant space-age polymer: scrap wood! Since we couldn't figure out how to make it round like a Mercury space capsule, we decided somehow that a triangular shape was aerodynamic. We built it with a hatch (more like a trap door) in the top with shiny brass hinges from Herwick's Hardware store. There was one problem. We ran out of lumber as we reached the top rear of the ship. Aha! Roofing tarpaper...that's space-like! We painted the outside white and silver (there was lots of silver paint laying around left over from painting pipes and radiators in the house).

Now it was time to work on the all-important interior. We brought blankets and lined the floor (which was fire-retardant for space travel), then added a few pillows for launch position. I had an old plastic dash from a racing-car game that I thought would be perfect for the ship's control panel. We lit it from behind with a few flashlights. Then we did some garbage picking. We found several damaged thermos bottle liners. We were so excited. We had found our oxygen tanks! We taped them inside of the "fuselage."

I think we flew somewhere in that ship everyday of summer vacation between second and third grade. Some days, Mom would bring lunch down and hand it to us through the hatch...on the household dinnerware. I tried to explain that astronauts don't eat on plates, so she started handing us our meals in the new kitchen invention—*plastic sandwich bags*—how space age! We also ate TV dinners. For those of you who do not remember the first Swanson TV dinners, they came in aluminum trays. Just like the astronauts, we thought!

We had spacesuits, too. Well, not really; just helmets. We wore re-tooled football helmets! Flights lasted a full day (with breaks for the bathroom, of course); a full day was defined from after breakfast to dinner. We "flew" the entire day; to distant planets and imaginary places, and seemed to leave the real world behind. What incredible journeys we made, at least in our own minds and fantasies. Each day, we were able to take ourselves, believably, to new worlds.

I had forgotten about the spaceship journeys until, as I said at the onset of this story, Don reminded me of them. I feel wonderful and unencumbered when I think of them. I believe that musicians need to revisit the times in their lives when they fantasized. That fantasy skill should be revisited time and time again so that the musician artist can take the journeys that great music requires of us. For those of us who teach, whether it is in the classroom or in the rehearsal room, it is important for us to relate our own experiences in childhood fantasy so that our musicians will gain access to a whole new world of musical expression.

Did you ever fly in a rocket ship, build a tree house, make a clubhouse, or play in refrigerator boxes? Refrigerator boxes are the stuff of great musicians! Don't you agree? Sit back, take a journey backwards in your life, smile, and enjoy the ride!

Author's Note: This story is written in deep appreciation of Donald W. Stoppi for the most valued friendship of my life. While we do not see or speak to each other often, Don is always in my thoughts. His kind and gentle spirit has had a great influence on my life.

a teacher speaks

Teaching, like any truly human activity, emerges from one's inwardness, for better or worse. As I teach, I project the condition of my soul onto my students, my subject, and our way of being together. The entanglements I experience in the classroom are often no more or less than the convolutions of my inner life. Viewed from this angle, teaching holds a mirror to the soul. If I am willing to look in that mirror and not run from what I see, I have a chance to gain self-knowledge—and knowing myself is as crucial to good teaching as knowing my students and my subject.

In fact, knowing my students and my subject depends heavily on self-knowledge. When I do not know myself, I cannot know who my students are. I will see them through a glass darkly, in the shadows of my unexamined life—and when I cannot see them clearly I cannot teach them well. When I do not know myself, I cannot know my subject—not at the deepest levels of embodied, personal meaning. I will know it only abstractly, from a distance, a congeries of concepts as far removed from the world as I am from personal truth. **(p. 2)**

Parker J. Palmer

The Courage to Teach

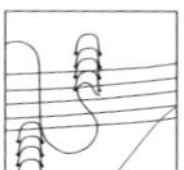

The claim that good teaching comes from the identity and integrity of the teacher might sound like a truism, and a pious one at that: good teaching comes from good people.

But by identity and integrity I do not mean only our noble features, or the good deeds we do, or the brave faces we wear to conceal our confusions and complexities. Identity and integrity have as much to do with our shadows and limits, our wounds and fears, as with our strengths and potentials. **(p. 13)**

How does one attend to the voice of the teacher (musician) within? I have no particular methods to suggest, other than the familiar bones: solitude and silence, meditative reading and walking in the woods, keeping a journal, finding a friend who will listen. I simply propose that we need to learn as many ways as we can of "talking to ourselves."

That phrase, of course, is one we normally use to name a symptom of mental imbalance—a clear sign of how culture regards the idea of the inner voice! But people who learn to talk to themselves may soon delight in the discovery that the teacher within is the sanest conversation partner they have ever had. **(p. 32)**

Parker J. Palmer

The Courage to Teach

February 26, 2001

Dr. James Jordan
Westminster Choir College
of Rider University
101 Walnut Lane
Princeton, NJ 08540

Dear James:

How can I express my gratitude and appreciation for you in mere words? This letter begins as a thank you for speaking to the UNT students and faculty last Thursday but it continues as much more. You touched the lives of everyone who heard either of your talks. It was exceedingly gracious of you to come early and offer your thoughts to us.

Your book *(The Musician's Soul)* has meant a great deal to me since I first read it last spring. I have passed it on to many students and friends, all of whom have been as enthusiastic as me about it. It was wonderful to hear you speak about the subject and to hear the examples from your own life. I can't tell you how encouraged I was by those stories of being "on the right side" and turning it around. As a teacher, I have approached most of my work from the left side instinctively (I had great teachers at an early age!). Many singers and voice teachers approach all of their endeavors from the other side. I have been told numerous times that I don't have enough competitive edge, or that I "care too much about the students." (I know that one of my references has said that if he had a negative comment about me as a teacher, it would be that I get too invested in the students.) When I first read your book, I knew that there were others who saw their profession as I did. In the book I found both reassurance for my own beliefs and clear instructions on how to continue to grow as a teacher and person.

Seeing you this past week and having the opportunity to

discuss various aspects of my career was incredibly rejuvenating for me. The academic life can be an emotional challenge, particularly at a school as large as this one. It was great to be able to discuss my concerns and to be reassured that I don't need to spend that kind of energy on them. Your visit couldn't have come at a better time for me emotionally. I truly appreciate all of the time you spent talking with me while you were here.

There is astonishing power in your ideas, as I found once again in the two lessons I taught on Friday after your lecture. The first student was a doctoral soprano who is currently teaching at Baylor (she's actually a little older than I am). She gets herself incredibly worked up about all of the wrong things, especially now that her recital is in three weeks; our big issue has been trying to release some of the tension and to enjoy singing once again. Towards the end of her lesson, I told her that she could easily sing all of the music on her program. She started to laugh derisively, and I said, "Don't you believe that you can sing all of this easily?" She immediately burst into tears and said no. I suggested to her that she doesn't need to worry about all of the little details at this point, and what she needed to do is believe that she can sing the program. Until she believed that, the rest of it was just cover. We had quite a discussion and all of her fears came out. The program would be quite different now!

The second student was the problem child I discussed at length with you. For once, she was not all dressed to the nines; she arrived in old overalls and a sweatshirt. I took one look at her face and knew that she was dreading this lesson. And why wouldn't she, after I had created such a difficult environment for her? I told her that I just wanted to talk today, because I wanted to make a new start. Before too long, tears were shed and all kinds of stories came out. It turns out that her parents divorced when she was very young and her father was largely absent after that. Apparently she's the mediator in her family, and there's not much warmth happening. Learning all of this about her changed my entire perspective. I had been thinking about removing her from my studio, but now I knew that a real teacher wouldn't give up on a student without really trying to know her. I realized that I had not allowed her to do her best work because I had not loved her as the others. I feel that a huge weight has been lifted!

I hope that we will keep in touch and that someday we might have the chance to work together again. Thank you for your beautiful soul and your thoughtful ideas that have changed so many lives.

All the very best,

Lynn Eustis, D.M.
Assistant Professor of Voice

Lynn Eustis, D.M.
Assistant Professor of Voice
University of North Texas College of Music
P.O. Box 311367
Denton, TX 76205
Leustis@music.unt.edu

beginning to unforget: re-storying influences

While I do not have extensive experience in other professions, I find that musicians have a strange sense of memory. Because most of their musical life is spent trying to "be in the moment," they spend little, if any, time re-storying their lives. While many areas of their lives fall into an abyss of memory loss, one I find peculiar is how musicians become incredibly proprietary with what they learn, even when others taught it to them lovingly. As time advances in their careers, they "forget" the persons who taught them, and stake claim on all that they know or do on their own genius and intuition.

One of the more fascinating things to read in the music profession is the professional biography of persons. As they should, those biographies talk of their musical achievements. I find, however, that I am always in for a great performance when I read about who taught them in their bios. Greats like Joshua Bell and Yo-Yo Ma always mention their teachers. But I find it interesting when I see musicians who never acknowledge their teachers. This is not a problem with appropriateness and acknowledgement; this is a symptom of someone who has lost contact with their life. Those who teach us are an incredible part of our lives. To not acknowledge that is a type of closure that is more profound that almost anything I know. It indicates not only a lack of appreciation, but a blatant disconnection to one's self.

Many of the stories in our lives are connected to those who taught us something. By saying "teachers," I do not only mean those who teach us about our craft, but those who teach us about our lives. Unfortunately, the lessons are never committed to our soulful existence until we acknowledge that they played a role in our lives. It is also an important part of re-storying our lives that we share with the world what they have taught us.

I find that musicians who are about themselves and become immersed in how incredibly gifted they are generally just that; very gifted. But because they do not re-story their lives, their gift never reaches its true depth in the music they perform. In their own world, *they* believe it does. Their false sense of reality is their biggest obstacle; yet they never understand it. Moreover, I have also found that persons who separate themselves from the teachers in their lives generally do so in order to increase their own self- esteem in their own eyes and/or the eyes of others.

When was the last time you thought about all the persons who taught you? If you have not begun this part of the re-storying process, the number of people who will come to the surface will stagger you. Why do we forget them? And, it is not the fact that we forget them, but we lose sight of the valuable things they taught us. To lose sight of this life-stuff is very detrimental to music making. It creates a deep, unnoticed closure. Access to valuable and hard-learned lessons is lost. And most importantly, the seeds of knowledge that were so lovingly planted within us are never watered, and never grow.

Many persons chalk all this up as immaturity. I attribute it to a lack of re-storying as a vital part of our growth process. One does not come into the world "gifted." One possesses gifts that are nurtured by people who love and care for others. That, perhaps, is the definition of a great teacher. To forget the messengers and the gifts they developed is to lose sight of the gift. The "gift" is a material piece of knowledge that becomes musically and psychologically crippling.

I have never forgotten the major teachers in my life. But I have forgotten some of the "minor" ones. In reality, the minor ones were not minor. Here is a *partial* list of these people, not in any particular order of chronology or importance.

John Scott
Gail Poch
Janet Yamron
Leslie Jarrett
David Milne
William Payn
Frederic Billman
Donald Stoppi
B. Stimson Carrow
Eve Meyer
Elizabeth Jordan
George Miller
James Steffy
Lawrence Cooper
Heidi Lynn
Helen Kemp
Joseph Flummerfelt
Barbara Conable
Allen Crowell
Kenneth Raessler
Christe Pyper
Catherinne Jarrett
Louis Jordan
Veronica Kryscio
Bernard Kunkel
Donald Beckie
Elaine Brown
Sarah Farley
Georgianna Kresl
Roger Ames
John Clifford
Matthew Mehaffey
Edwin Gordon
Heather Buchanan
Jeffrey Bruce
Roger Dean
Catherine Payn
Eric Kephart
Phyllis Bressler
Rita Richard
Frederic Jarrett
Lori Ann Jordan
Robert W. Baker
Bede Camera
Daniel Payn
H. Christopher Ross
Calvin Borgeault
Florence Jordan
Mark Kelleher
James Boeringer

You try this drill. You begin a list like I did. Floods of memories *and* information about music and life come flooding back. It puts you in touch with the richness of your life, and the sheer depth of your experience. By re-storying in such a way, how could you not influence your music?

After you have made your list pondered what your teachers taught you, take the exercise to a higher level. Try to recall how they taught you. For it is in this aspect of their sharing that they have profoundly affected you. It is not what they taught you, but *how* they taught you. In all cases, you will begin to understand how love and care figure into the teaching/learning process.

To those of you reading this who have not thought about those who have taught you, begin anew. By re-storying in such a manner, I believe you deepen yourself and access many areas of knowledge that you have forgotten about, or have simply claimed as your own "intuition." To re-acknowledge persons is a way to connect or perhaps re-connect to so many things that make your life your unique event. By re-storying, the teachers who taught you will provide a newfound depth to your art.

VI
a musician's guide
to achieving mindfulness

As we work on opening the heart, we will confront, over and over, our fearful habit of closing to pain. This is where mindfulness meditation practice can be such a powerful ally and a wonderful companion as we sail the seas of the heart. It keeps us focused and less likely to be swept away by waves of elation or despair. Mindfulness and heart-fulness are a powerful duo to a spiritual path: a quiet mind without an open heart is a pretty brittle and boring proposition. But an open heart that doesn't have the support of a quiet and tamed mind is equally unhelpful. Without spirituality, therapy can turn into a never-ending search for self-fulfillment. Without heartfulness, spiritual practice can lead us away from the gifts of life. **(p. 160)**

Elizabeth Lesser

The New American Spirituality

Before rehearsals or performance, it is often incredibly beneficial to develop a routine for meditation or accessing what Zen practitioners refer to as "mindfulness." Mindfulness can only be accessed through quiet and breathing. Since most of what we do as musicians is intricately connected to the breath, meditative sequences that require us to quiet ourselves before musical activity can be beneficial. These can be done in the rehearsal room or in the office. Location is not important. Setting the time, however, is important. A few minutes of mindfulness focus can provide access to a great musical reservoir within you.

achieve quiet

Random thoughts dash through our conscious mind. Psychologists called these dashing thoughts "monkey brain." The only way to quiet "monkey brain" is by accessing some degree of mindfulness through breath. It is important to gain distance from your thoughts. Imagine that you have placed yourself in an observational place; a tower, a high building, and that you are looking down or in the very far distance at your thoughts. Put *distance* between you and your thoughts.

achieve body balance

Be skilled at gaining optimum alignment in your body as you sit. When aligned properly, the body feels as if it is doing no work. Think of lengthening and widening your back. Make sure that you have a correct map of your body. To do this, learn the six points of balance from the book titled, *The Structures and Mechanisms of Breathing* by Barbara Conable (GIA Publications, Inc.).

soften while you align

As you lengthen your spine, soften your abdomen. Soften your abdomen and concentrate on opening your heart. Become *awake and aware.* Be aware of every square inch of your body, which will bring you into a heightened sense of awareness of your body and the world.

breathe

Allow breath to be the connector between your body, your mind, and your spirit. Be devoid of dashing "monkey brain" thoughts. If "monkey brain" still exists, concentrate on your breath to bring you into mindfulness. The breath will help *distance* you from those unnecessary thoughts.

accept life and its difficulties

In distancing yourself from dashing, interfering thoughts, be careful to acknowledge the painful parts of your life. Pain, sorrow, anguish, and troubles are part of life. Accept them, and make them safe and manageable. Acknowledge that these things are present in your life and place them in proper perspective for your meditative, spiritual life: in the background. By doing this, you will keep them as part of your experience, but in proper perspective. Left unattended, they tend to overtake one's all-important want to access mindfulness.

practice mindfulness daily

Do this procedure daily. The length of time is not important, but frequency is. Frequent repetitions of this practice will allow entrance into mindfulness quickly and easily. Also, practice mindfulness throughout your day; do not limit it to a need before music making.

access the correct mimesis

In *The Musician's Soul,* I detailed the importance of a correct mimetical place in all that one does. Remember, one must make the correct conscious choice to be in the right place: a loving, caring place at all times. The access of this loving, caring place is of paramount importance for musicians and artists. Rid yourself of all forms of anger and self-doubt. Love yourself first, then love for others will follow. Honest music making will be the result. Refer to the Mimetic Chapter in *The Musician's Soul* for further guidance. The Meditation audiotape that accompanies *The Musician's Soul* can be of great assistance in this process.

expect resistance

The "monkeys" will visit you and try to disrupt your mindfulness time. The "monkeys' assume the disguises of life pains, restlessness, sleepiness, doubts, self-criticism, and self-mutilation. Use conscious choice to stay in a "good" and loving place. Conscious choice, repeated over again, is the best antidote to mindful static. In addition to good mimetical thoughts, use your breath to quiet the "monkeys."

Musician's Spirit

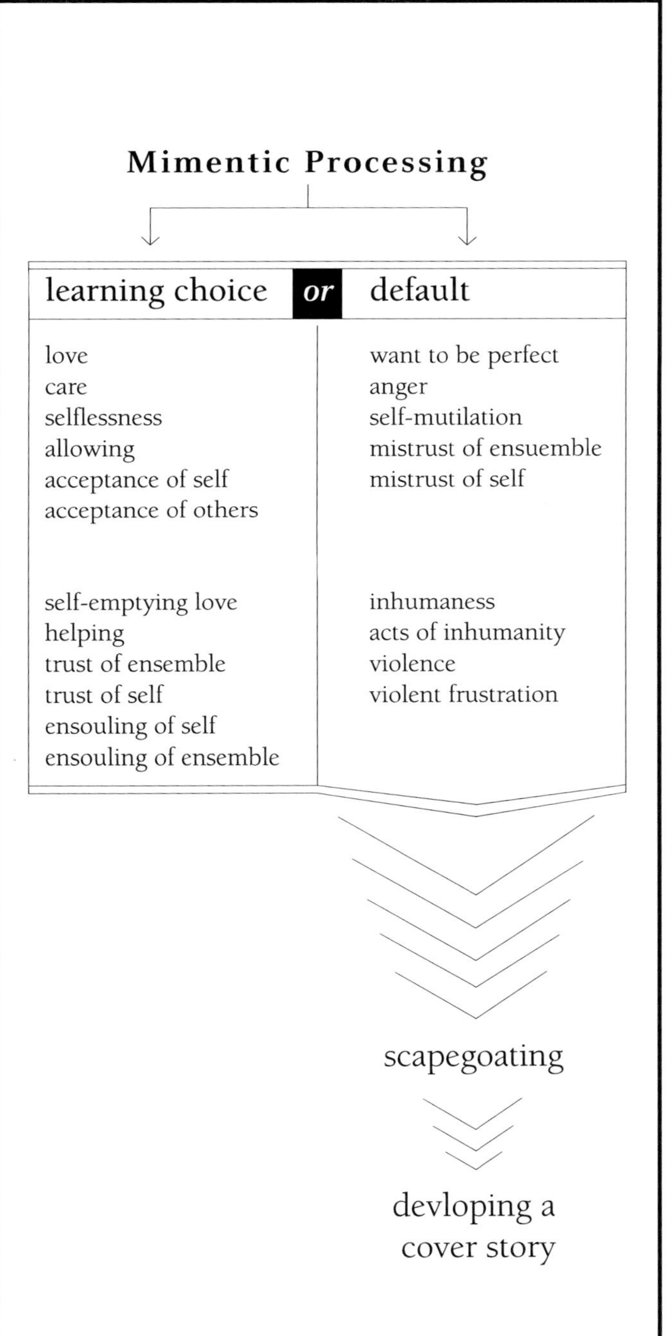

listen to your breath

As you still and calm your inner and outer self, listen to your breath. Listening to breath is the best practice for listening skills that are necessary in music making. If you can quiet yourself and hear *that* quiet, you will begin to gain the same skills that you need to use when listening as a musician. Many times, when the mental "monkeys" begin to jump, breath and your awareness of it is the only way to connect with yourself.

learn to enjoy stillness and the quiet passing of time

Enjoy the relative stillness of gently passing time. Enjoy the slowness and calm of passing time when viewed and accessed from mindfulness. It is out of this quiet acknowledgement of stillness from which a musician's sense of consistent tempo is grown and nurtured.

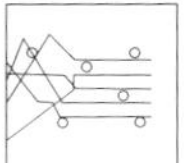

When we direct spiritual attention to the heart, we take our practice to the next step. In the Landscape of the Mind we sit boldly in reality, just as it is, with no judgment or fear, no likes or dislikes—just awareness (p.157)

If the purpose of life is to 'feel the rapture of being alive,' and if our capacity to feel is crippled by old wounds and a lack of emotional education, then it follows that an important part of the spiritual path is to heal the heart and to become emotionally intelligent. Then why is it that the territory of the heart is so rarely explored on the classical spiritual journey? One answer is that contradictory, messy, passionate nature seems at odds with some religions. Sin-based religions especially have made it their mission to control the world, not to love it for what it is. The less controllable aspects of our humanness—erotic love, rage and anger, beauty and sadness—have been labeled too passionate or irrational to be trusted. Better to leave passion out of a 'spiritual' person's life altogether. **(p. 160)**

Elizabeth Lesser

The New American Spirituality

conclusion

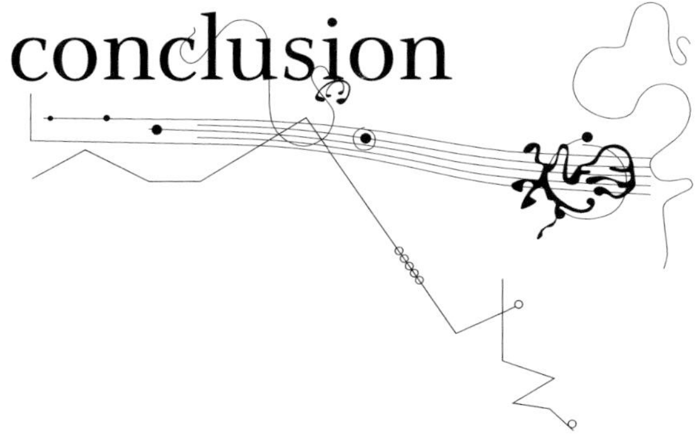

guide to developing narrative and storying skills

There is a peculiar gap between our lives and ourselves. I have conceived this gap in terms of a variety of oppositions. It is a gap between our existence and our experience, and between our experience and our expression. It is a gap between the facts of life and the artifacts we form from them in memory and imagination. It is a gap between living and telling, between biology and biography, between development and emplotment, between nature and character, and between life and life-story. **(p. 328)**

William Lowell Randall

The Stories We Are

Developing Story through Scripting

The ability to tell stories may be a natural ability in some. In others, it may take some development of technique and style. I have found that the following exercise is useful toward such an end.

Go out and listen in on a conversation between two or more persons. Transcribe the conversation as close as you can remember it. Reconstruct the dialogue like a script. This exercise works best with two or more people. After the dialogue/script is reconstructed, give your script to another person to "read." Set no guidelines for the reading of your "mini-script." Read it as you wish; interpret it as you like. Read it several times.

You will discover that you'll develop story-telling skills with this exercise. What begins as a simple reading develops into a creative narrative technique, or a way of retelling a story. Reading aloud can also develop this technique. It is important that one is comfortable telling and sharing ideas. It is sometimes easier to begin with material that is not personally connected to you, then eventually, you will develop a story-telling technique that is reflective of your soul.

Re-telling Your Story: The Musician's New Journey

The role of storying can play an important role in the music-making process. The relationship you have with your own life is important in order to develop a metaphor of the life as story. It is almost like a Pandora's box of sorts. As we lift its cover, play with the contents, and peer into our "story

Musician's Spirit

box," we re-discover events in our lives that hold profound human meaning and serve as metaphors for the music and art we create. Our life then becomes an unfolding novel, and we can draw from the narrator, the main protagonist, and the reader. Re-storying, in essence, enables us to author ourselves into being. It is that revisited being which provides a treasure rove of inspiration for ourselves, and hopefully, others with whom we make music. It must also be realized that you not only have a story, but you are the story.

This process is about self-creation through the process of telling your own story. Many musicians move through their lives unaware of their own story, yet desperately want to make meaningful music. I am proposing what I believe to be a powerful paradigm for use in both the classroom and the rehearsal. Not until you re-story yourself and bring yourself into being will you have the necessary stuff for music making. Some of the re-storying can be told to help music that, through its message, has inspired life experiences. For many other pieces, your story remains silently within you. That silent re-storying will provide you with an interior depth unknown to you and the people with whom you make music. You will find a whole new reservoir of life available for use in your music making.

storying guide

The guide below is meant to be exactly that: a guide. What is most important is that you take the leap into telling yourself your own story! I think you will be amazed at how much of your life experiences you have forgotten. They have become buried amid the whirl of your adult life. I also believe that revisiting all aspects of your early life will bring you newfound joy and happiness, and ultimately, a clarifying of the life experience. That re-constituted life is the one that will prove to be invaluable for your music making. The more time you spend thinking about and answering the questions below, the more you will learn about yourself. My suggestion is that you purchase a journal and write your responses to these questions in it. Use the spaces below to create an outline. Expand on the outline below in a formal journal book. Revisit the questions and their answers often and re-work them as time and wisdom require. Another suggestion is that you sift through photo albums. Photos have a remarkable way of spawning forgotten memories and life stories.

I have another suggestion. After writing down your "story," go back and read it through, and place yourself in the role of a narrator. Speak your story out loud to yourself. Such "narrative" work develops the storytelling skill that is necessary in the music classroom or rehearsal room. Finally, read your story again, this time focusing on it as a reader. Analyze it and re-live it. Experience it again. I believe by doing this you will discover even more stories that will be an outgrowth of what you have written.

One final caution. Do not be surprised if there is a gap between yourself and your life. Existence versus actual life experiences tends to build huge walls within people, especially artists. By storying, you begin to break down this wall, which I believe limits creativity and music making. That barrier also limits or inhibits fantasy and wonder—the most valuable tools for a musician at *any level.*

Musician's Spirit

What kind of Story will you tell? What is the title of your Story?

What is the Major theme of your story?

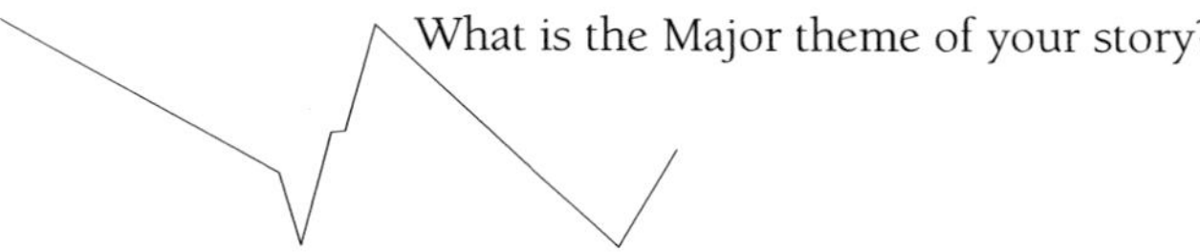

Have you ever told your life story to anyone?
If you have, does it change with each telling?
Why?

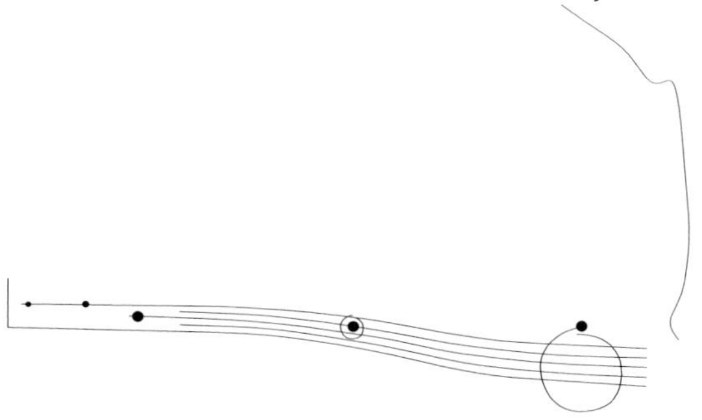

Describe yourself as the major "character" in your story.

How do you describe yourself?

In telling your story, spend a considerable amount of time on your childhood. It is during childhood that most human emotions needed in music making are experienced for the first time. Those experiences also tend to be relatively isolated from other emotions, and hence, are more easily accessible.

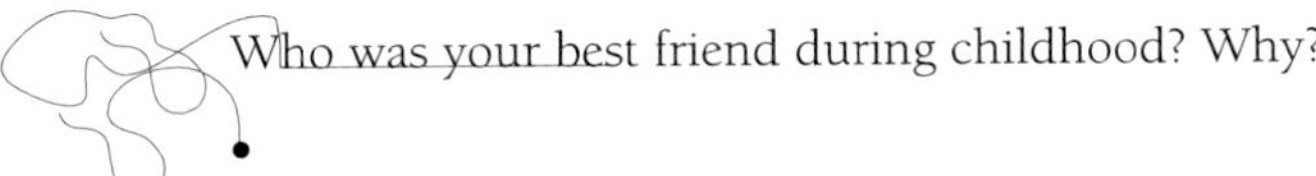
Who was your best friend during childhood? Why?

What experiences did you share with
that friend that shaped your life?

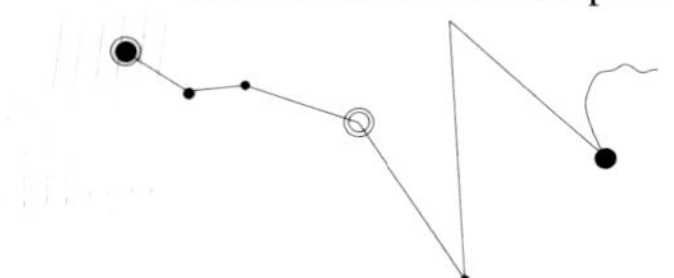

Is there anyone who could serve as your official biographer?
Why?

Who are the heroes in your life story?
Why?

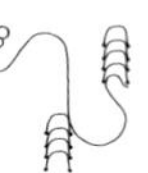

How many chapters are there in your life story?
List the titles of the chapters below.

Are there any recurring themes in your life?

What are the major learning experiences of your life?
Who were the "teachers" who taught them to you?
Did they share any similar characteristics?

What was or are the defining historical
events that occurred in your life?
How did those events affect your soul?

Is there any event in your life, which
can be considered a turning
point?

When was the first time in your life that you realized you had a "soul" or a type of "soulfulness?"

Is there anyone who knows your "story?" If the answer is no, why?

Are there any heroes in your story? Who and Why?

Write about three of the most *Joyful* events of your life.

James Jordan

Write about three life situations in which
you were in a desperate state.

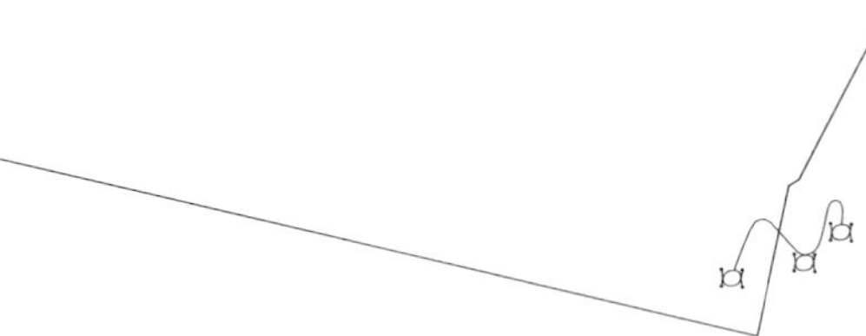

Write about three situations where you were
the RECIPIENT of love outside of a personal relationship.

Musician's Spirit

Write about three situations or events where you shared love with another outside of a personal relationship.

Write about FIVE situations in you life where you were angry. Please write if the anger was ever resolved.

Describe
five
events
in
your
life
where
you
visually
perceived
beauty.

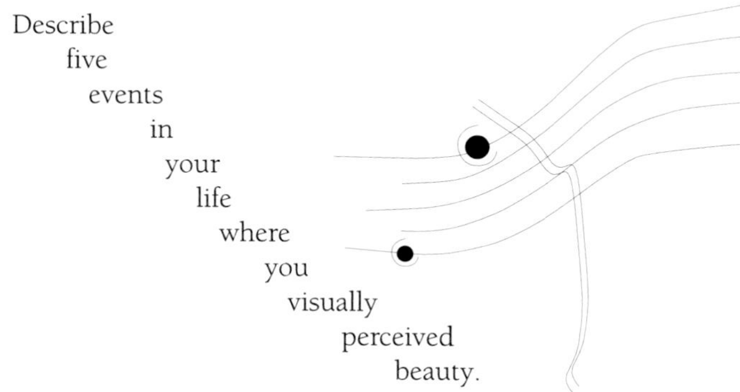

Write about three times when you learned about the
necessity for solitude and quiet.

Musician's Spirit

Describe events in your life, which have taught you and led you to understand your spirituality.

Who are the most spiritual people in your life and why do they play such a role?

Describe your first PROFOUND musical experience.

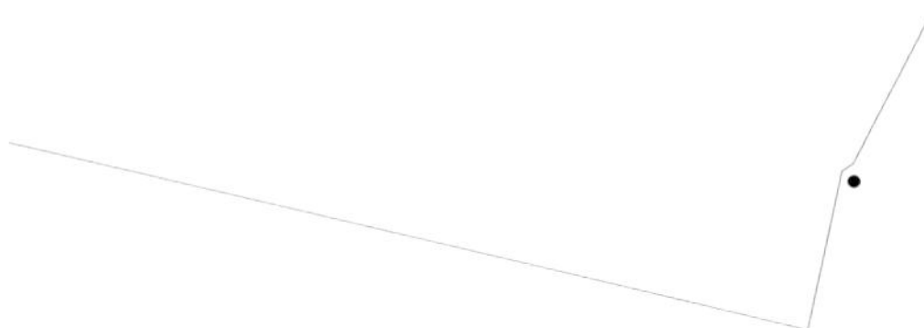

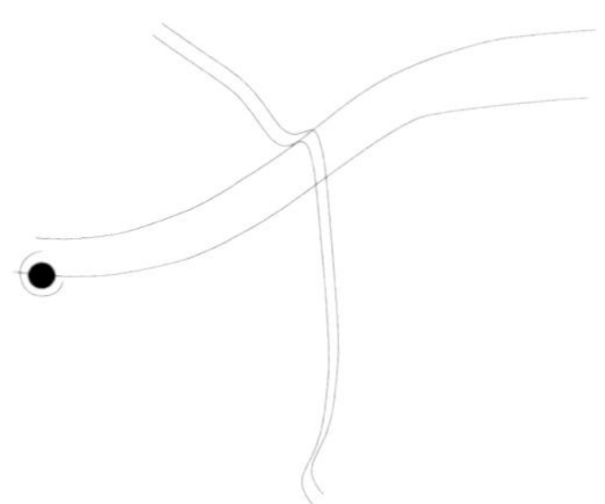

Musician's Spirit

Describe the most profound religious experience in your life.

Discuss a person in your life who has passed away. Why was that person such a profound influence?

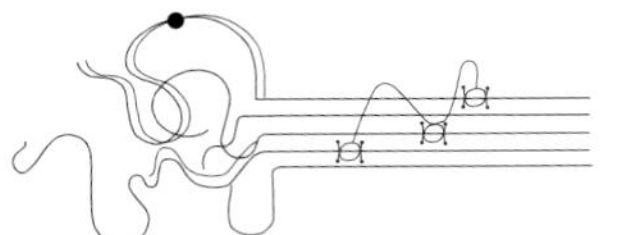

Write about the influence of your mother on your life.

Discuss the role of your father in your life.

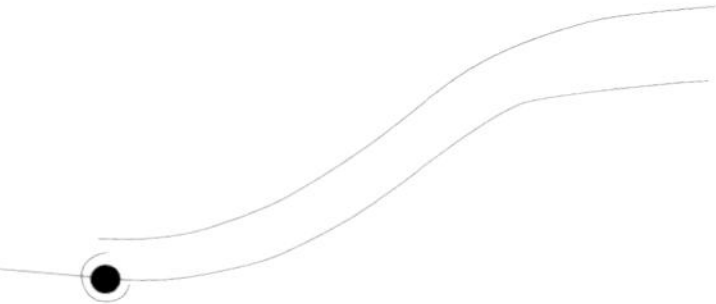

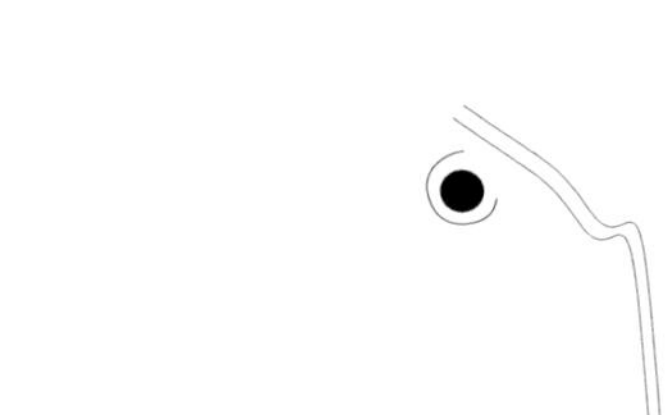

Musician's Spirit

Discuss your relationships with your siblings.

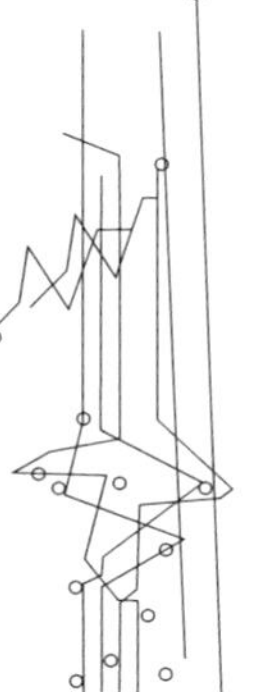

List five students or professional colleagues who have had a deep and lasting influence on you.

Discuss situations in your life where you felt discriminated. How did you handle those discriminatory events?

Musician's Spirit

What was your first experience with death?
How did you handle that first experience?

Write about yours views concerning death.
Have you ever confronted death?

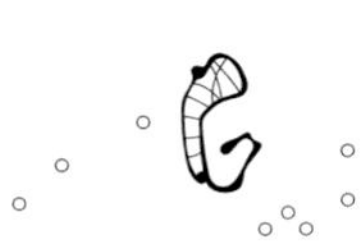

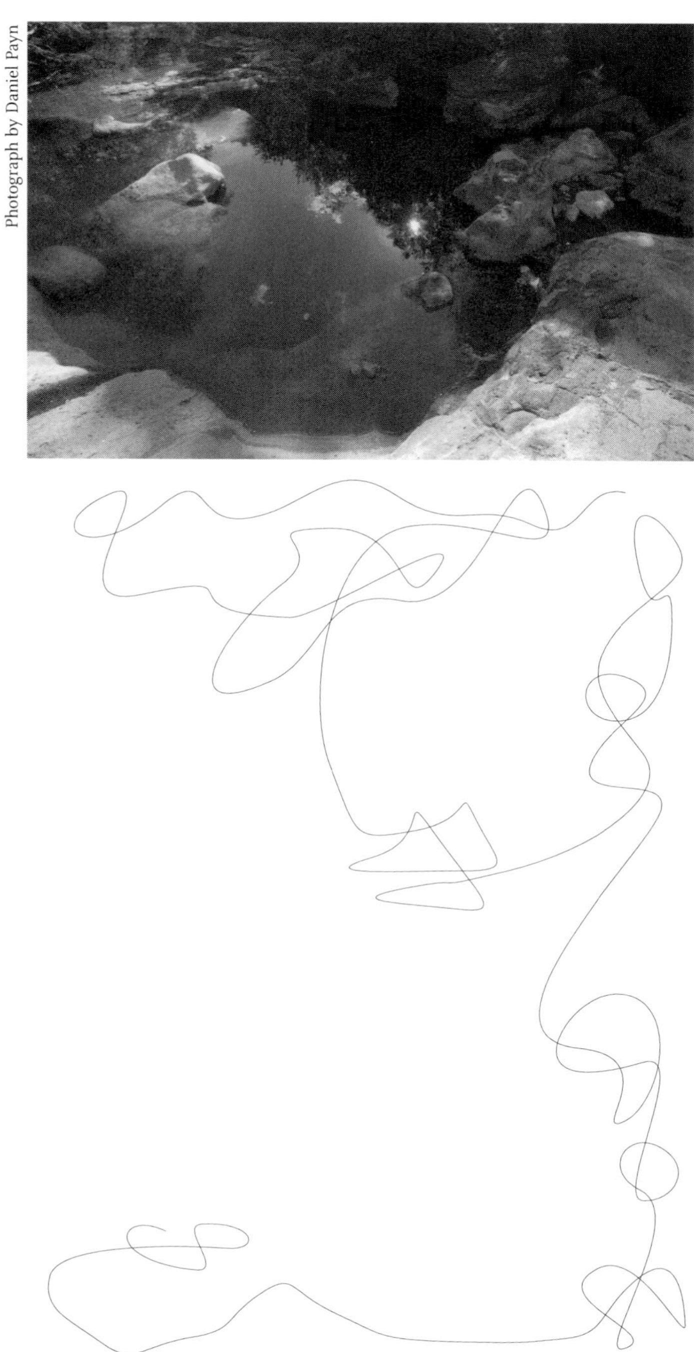

Photograph by Daniel Payn

Search your photo albums.

Paste in photos of the happiest moments of your life.

What music are you studying at this point? What are are the universal themes in that music? What experiences from your life could help bring you closer to that music?

Who were the major teachers in your life?

For each person on the above list what each person taught you.

After thinking about WHAT each person taught you, think about HOW they taught it to you.

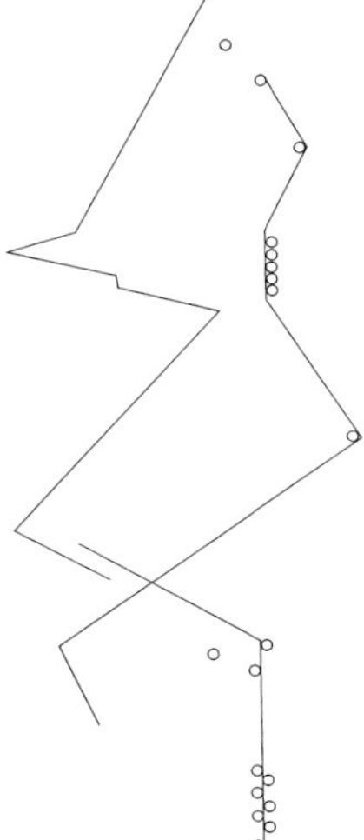

Musician's Spirit

How has your "tem permanent" affected your life storying?
Has your temperament changed throughout your life? Why?

Has your gender played a role in the re-storying of your life?

James Jordan

What role has calm and quiet played in your life?

Of all your life stories, which chapters rely your essence?
Can these essential stories play a role in connecting music
to you?

Musician's Spirit

words to assist in the storying journey: provoking meaning through seizing the teachable moment

A man is always a teller of tales;

He lives surrounded by his stories and

The stories of others; he sees everything

That happens to him through them,

And he tries to live his life as

If he were recounting it.

Jean-Paul Sarte

Nausea

Storying is living and dynamic.

Stories exist to be exchanged.

They are the currency of human growth.

Jean Houston

The Search for the Beloved

Strictly speaking, there is no time when we are not living in 'the vale of soul-making,' for we are continually re-storying our souls. Our stories are never the same. Not only is my story different from your story, but technically, it is different from the story it was a decade ago, a day ago, or only and hour ago. They change, if for no other reason than because with each passing year, day, or hour they get longer, which means there are literally more events in them—or at least more events to be made into them potentially. There are more events in them at the level not only of existence or outside story but of experience as well, the level of the inside story. There are more events that we have digested, transformed, or 'made,' through some imaginative process, 'intro' experiences. **(p. 234-235)**

William Lowell Randall

The Stories We Are

Bidden or Not Bidden

God is Present

Carl Jung

Carved above the Office Door

Spirituality is always at risk of becoming anorexic. The word means no appetite, and indeed spiritual teachings often seem frustrated with human appetites. **(p.229)**

Thomas Moore

The Soul's Religion

Part of the challenge of story is two-fold. First you must awaken your story in your life memory, then travel to that place in your memory and retrieve the story so that it can be told. Stated in another way, how can we provoke or prod our most intimate life memories? For choral musicians, words carry meaning. For instrumentalists, words can stimulate the profound meaning of the music and cause us to connect more intimately with the composer's voice. Many times, in connecting a story to music, it is helpful to have a word or phrase that will cause your storying "thinking" to proceed in certain directions. In addition to evoking sound from music, it is also our mission to provoke meaning from the text.

However, most times, one can access a great trove of stories through life's memory; through simple remembering, a miracle of the human experience. But it is sometimes difficult, if not impossible, to articulate to an ensemble or another group of musicians the basic human truth that the music contains in a poignant, well-chosen word that will cause the musicians to take the journey with you, and hence, gain a profound understanding of the piece of music you are rehearsing. The exact word at the exact moment in a rehearsal can catapult many into your journey. Such words sometimes contain a key to what I call the "storying code," or words that can unlock the mind's rich life experience. Once the semantics are right, a whole new world of human connection through feeling can be unlocked and shared.

These words, however, can serve another very important function. During score study, it is important to try to hear the voice of the composer, and try to ascertain what profound human truths are contained within the sounds of the piece. As a performer or conductor, it is pivotal to rehearsal and performance that the conductor embarks on the journey that the composer traveled. There is a danger that for the sake of expediency, interpreters of the score hastily "apply" his or her story onto a score without careful consideration of the composer's intent. When this is done, the work becomes a shallow and dishonest. Your story should help the journey that the composer has provided, and not be in opposition of it.

Through score study and profound listening, a composer's "human intent" will become clear. It is at that point that you make your storying journey to access the life experience that can illuminate the basic human truths that the composer is trying to communicate. When you have arrived at all these decisions, it is important to have selected the exact word that will cause, almost instantaneously, you and your fellow musicians to take a storying journey that is intimately related to the composer's human intent.

A well-chosen word can be the password for your journey while rehearsing, and can then provide at the appropriate moment in the rehearsal process a password to your fellow musicians that will propel them on their own storying trajectory. Pope John Paul II called such events "teachable moments." The great musician can "read the room" and innately know what is a teachable moment. Those teachable moments are those times when, because of the course of a rehearsal through story, we are able and willing to hear what

Musician's Spirit

may be old things anew. Or in some cases, hear them for the first time. Essentially, such well-chosen words can provoke human beings into a meaningful state.

Each section of the score should have a word or phrase written on its pages that will serve as a constant reminder of what the music is "about" at that point. Those words must be pre-determined so that one can grasp such "teachable moments" in a rehearsal. Such words have an incredible emotional crystallizing process upon the interpretative act. Sometimes, in fact, many times, a well-chosen word can bring human truth and honesty into the music-making process. It is such "truth-seeking" which is so often absent in the rehearsal process and in many musical performances. Human truth in performance knows no barriers. It should be in a children's choir, a church choir, the high school choir, or the professional choir. The storying journey cannot be avoided if the music comes alive through the musical intent of the composer.

It goes without saying that such searching of the human spirit through storying is both time consuming and difficult. Many times, it must be teased from our memory. That is the purpose of the list that follows. But the rewards of a group of persons taking a journey together through word and story is one of the most valuable rehearsal techniques that one can possibly learn. To teach an ensemble that life is truly inseparable from the human story is, perhaps, the single most important objective of the rehearsal process. Essentially, it is the philosophical umbrella of the rehearsal process under which everything else about the rehearsal resides.

You must remember one basic truth about storying. While the details and events of our individual stories may vary, there is a commonality of common shared experience in all our stories. Storying is the vehicle by which humankind attempts to make meaning out of life. The objective of rehearsal is to arrive at a common story, which is the music. Understanding musical interpretation allows us to both individually and communally remember. By recalling life lived, we deepen our emotional imagination, and the palate of life opens itself to us. All of this serves as our emotional "re-education." Life itself has provided the initial indoctrination. We need to simply access what we have experienced. Hopefully the process suggested here will place life closer at hand, and make it an integral part of the music-making process; not an infinitely, remote-inaccessible "thing."

Such is the "stuff" of ordinary wisdom. But it is honest, ordinary wisdom that brings truth to music. The constant fluctuation of life between suspense and ambiguity is inherent in musical scores. Clarity, however, can be brought to life's stories through recall. Also, remember that no story is innocent. Even the most simple of Grandma's bedtime stories may drive home a human truth at a poignant and well-selected point in the rehearsal or score preparation process.

It is through that recall of life's stories that we become very wise. Truth begets truth over and over. Those truths should take permanent residence in the art we both perform and live. We should also be constantly vigilant for those "teachable moments" that will provoke both the music and us to an even higher ground.

storying codes and cue words

This list can serve two purposes. (1) For each word on this list, jot down a phrase that will serve as a cue to recall an experience from your life. When completed, this can serve as one of your most valuable resources. (2) After score study, select words from this list that summarize the human intent of the music. These chosen words can serve two purposes. First, to cause you to locate your spiritual place from which to perform the music, and secondly, to cause ensemble members to take a similar journey during rehearsal.

Abandoned
Abhor
Abiding
Abominable
Abrasive
Absolving
Absorbed
Absurd
Abused
Abusive
Accommodating
Acknowledged
Acquiescent
Acrimonious
Admonished
Adoration
Adored
Adventurous
Adverse
Affected
Affectionate
Afflicted
Affronted
Afraid
Aggravated
Aggressive
Agitated
Agonized
Agony
Agreeable
Airy
Awkward
Alienated
Alive
Alluring
Alone
Altruistic
Ambiguous
Ambitious
Amenable
Amorous
Amused
Anger
Angry
Anguished
Animated
Anonymous
Annoyed
Anxiety
Anxious
Apathy
Appealing
Appeasing
Appetizing
Appreciation
Apprehensive
Ardent
Arduous
Argumentative
Armored
Aroused
Arrogant
Ashamed
Astounded
Assurance
Attentive
Avoidance
Awe
Bare
Barren
Beaten down
Belief
Bemused
Betrayed
Bewildered

Bewitched
Bitter
Blessed
Blissful
Blunt
Boiling
Bored
Bothered
Brave
Breathless
Breezy
Bright
Brilliant
Broken
Bruised
Bucolic
Buoyant
Burdensome
Burnish
Bursting
Callous
Calm
Captivated
Captivating
Care
Careless
Caring
Cathartic
Celebrate
Celebrating
Chagrined
Chaotic
Charity
Charmed
Charming
Chastened
Cheerful
Cherishing
Childlike
Clandestine
Clear
Cold
Collected
Comfortable
Compassion
Competitive
Complacent
Completed
Composed
Concerned
Confused
Congenial
Content
Cool
Copacetic
Coping
Cordial
Cornered
Creative
Crucified
Crushed
Cursed
Cushy
Cut down
Dainty
Defensive
Dejected
Delectable
Delicate
Delighted
Demure
Depressed
Desirable
Desired
Desolate
Despair
Desperate
Despondent
Devoted
Devoured
Disbelief
Discomfort
Discontented
Disgust
Dismal
Dispassionate
Displeased
Disregard
Disregarding
Dissolved
Distracted
Distressed
Disturbed
Doldrums
Doomed
Dull
Eager
Earthly
Earnest
Easy
Ecstatic
Electric
Embracing
Enchanted
Endearing
Endure
Enduring
Enfolding
Engaging
Enjoy
Enlivened
Enraged
Enraptured
Enthused
Enthusiastic
Enticing
Eternal
Even tempered
Exacerbated
Exasperated
Excited
Exciting
Excluded
Exultation
Faith
Faithfulness
Fanatical
Fascinated
Fascinating

Fear
Fearful
Fearing
Fervent
Fervor
Fiery
Flared up
Flattering
Flicker
Fluid
Flushed
Flustered
Foolish
Foolhardy
Forebode
Forbearance
Fortitude
Frantic
Fracture
Fretful
Frigid
Frisky
Frustration
Full
Fulfilled
Fuming
Fun
Funny
Furious
Galvanized
Genial
Give
Giving
Glad
Glee
Gleeful
Glitter
Glisten
Gloom
Gloomy
Glorious
Glowing
Gnawing
Good
Goodness
Grateful
Gratified
Gratitude
Grave
Grief
Grieving
Grim
Gripping
Grounded
Haggard
Half-hearted
Hardened
Harsh
Hearty
Heavy
Hectic
Hilarious
Holy
Hope
Hopeful
Horrific
Horrified
Horror-stricken
Hostile
Hovering
Humble
Humbling
Humorous
Hurt
Hysterical
Illusion
Illuminating
Impetuous
Imposing
Impressed
Impressionable
Impulsive
In a flurry
In a stupor
In a trance
In purgatory
Inattentive
Inclusive
Indulged
Indulgent
Inept
Inexhaustible
Infelicitous
Inflexible
Infuriated
Insatiable
Insensitive
Insouciant
Inspired
Inspirited
Interested
Intimidated
Intrigued
Intuitive
Invite
Inviting
Inward
Irrepressible
Irritated
Irritation
Jaunty
Jealous
Jittery
Jolly
Jovial
Joy
Joyful
Joyous
Jubilation
Languid
Languish
Laugh
Laughingly
Lethargic
Light hearted
Liquid
Lively
Loathe
Lonely

Lonesome
Long-suffering
Lost
Love
Loved
Loving
Lukewarm
Luxurious
Mad
Manic
Martyr
Melancholy
Merry
Mindful
Mindless
Mirthful
Miserable
Moderate
Mortified
Moved
Murky
Nervous
Nonchalant
Not caring
Numb
Optimistic
On the edge
Overflowing
Over-wrought
Pain
Panic
Paralyzed
Passionate
Passive
Patient
Peace of mind
Perky
Perplexed
Perturbation
Perturbed
Petrified
Pine
Piquant
Pitied
Placid
Plagued
Playful
Pleasant
Pleasing
Pleasurable
Pleasure
Poignant
Pressured
Prey to
Pride
Protected
Proud
Provocative
Provoked
Quarrelsome
Quenched
Quiet
Quivering
Quivery
Radiant
Rash
Raving
Ravished
Ravishing
Receptive
Reckless
Reconciled
Redemptive
Redemption
Refreshed
Rejected
Rejection
Rejoice
Relish
Repressed
Repugnant
Rescued
Resentful
Resentment
Resigned
Resistant
Restrained
Restraint
Revived
Ridiculous
Romantic
Safe
Satiated
Satisfaction
Satisfied
Scared
Secretive
Secure
Sedate
Seduced
Seductive
Seething
Selfish
Sensational
Sensual
Sentimental
Serious
Shaken
Shielded
Shocked
Shutter
Shy
Silly
Simmering
Sincere
Sinking
Smug
Snug
Sob
Sober
Sobering
Soft
Solemn
Somber
Sore
Sorrow
Sorrowful
Sour
Sparkle

Sparkling
Spastic
Spicy
Spirited
Spry
Stark
Stoic
Stranded
Stressed
Stricken
Static
Stung
Stunned
Subdued
Subjugated
Suffer
Suffering
Sunny
Supportive
Surrender
Susceptible
Suspended
Sweet
Sympathy
Taken advantage of
Tame
Tantalizing
Temperate
Tender
Terrified
Threatened
Thrilled
Tickled
Tight
Tight-lipped
Timid Tingly
Tolerant
Tormented
Tortured
Touched
Transfixed
Transparent
Tranquil
Translucent
Transported
Trepidation
Troubled
Trust
Twitchy
Uncomfortable
Unconcerned
Unconscious
Uncontrollable
Under pressure
Undone
Unfeeling
Unhappy
Unimpressed
Unruffled
Valiant
Vexed
Victim
Victimized
Vivacious
Volcanic
Voluptuous
Vulnerable
Wail
Warm
Warmhearted
Weary
Welcomed
Whining
Wish
Winsome
Wistful
Woe
Woeful
Worldly
Worried
Wounded
Wretched
Yearn
Yearning
Yielding
Zeal
Zealous

notes, stories and reflections

This is your space to write your stories and record notes and personal reflections. In many ways, these can be the most valuable part of this book.

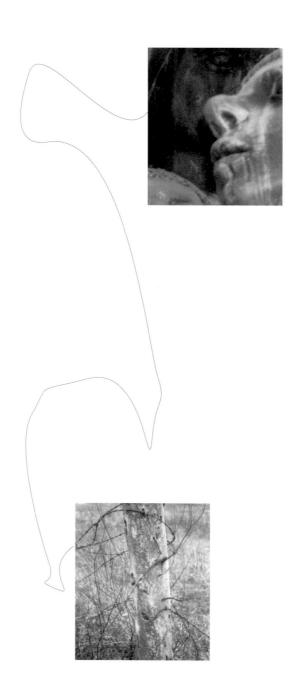

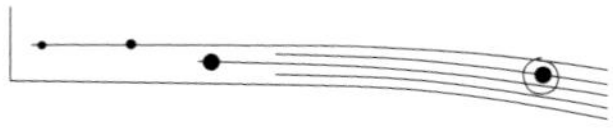

bibliography and suggested readings

Adolphe, Bruce. *What to Listen For In The World.* New York: Limelight Editions, 1996.

Albom, Mitch. *Tuesdays with Morrie.* New York: Doubleday, 1997.

Angelou, Maya. *A Song Flung Up To Heaven.* New York Random House, 2002.

Armstrong, Lane. *It's Not About The Bike: My Journey Back To Life.* New York: Berkley Books, 2001.

Barks, Coleman. *The Soul of Rumi: A New Collection of Ecstatic Poems.* San Francisco: Harper, 2001.

Barone, Tom. *Touching Eternity.* New York: Columbia University Press, 2001.

Battisti, Frank. "Rehearsing for a Musical Life." *The Instrumentalist,* 47, p. 84-92.

Beevers, John. Trans. *The Autobiography of Saint Therese of Liseaux: The Story of a Soul.* New York: Doubleday, 1957.

Bennett-Goleman, Tara. *Emotional Alchemy.* New York: Harmony Books, 2001.

Bernstein, Leonard. *Findings. Fifty Years of Meditations on Music.* New York: Doubleday, 1982.

Bernstein, Leonard. *The Joy of Music.* New York: Simon and Schuster, 1959.

Black Elk, Nicholas. *Black Elk Speaks.* Lincoln: University of Nebraska Press, 1932.

Bloom, H. *The Anxiety of Influence.* Oxford: Oxford University Press, 1973.

Bonhoffer, Dietrich. *Letters and Papers from Prison.* New York: Collier Books, 1971.

Boulding, Maria. Trans. *The Confessions of St. Augustine.* Hyde Park, NY: New City Press, 1997.

Boyda, Erza. *Being Zen.* Boston: Shambahala Publishers, 2002.

Briggs, C. *Learning How To Ask.* Cambridge: Cambridge University Press, 1986.

Brokaw, Tom. *An Album of Memories.* New York: Random House, 2001.

Bruner, Jerome. *Actual Minds, Possible Worlds.* Cambridge, Massachusetts: Harvard University Press, 1986.

Bryan, Mark. *The Artist's Way at Work.* New York: William Morrow and Co., 1998.

Bridges, W. *Transition: Making Sense of Life's Changes.* Toronto: Addison-Wesley, 1980.

Buber, Martin. *I and Thou.* New York: Scribner, 1970.

Buber, Martin. *Between Man and Man.* New York: Macmillan, 1965.

Buber, Martin. *The Prophetic Faith.* New York: Harper and Row, 1948.

Buber, Martin. *Two Types of Faith.* New York: Harper & Row Publishers, 1961.

Cameron, Julia. *The Artist's Way.* New York: G. Putman's Sons, 1992.

Carrington, Patricia. *Learn to Meditate.* Boston: Element Books, 1998.

Castaneda, Carlos. *The Wheel of Time.* Los Angeles: LA Eidolona Press, 1998.

Chodron, Pema. *The Places That Scare You.* Boston: Shambhala, 2000.

Clark, Hiro. (Ed.) *Picasso: In His Words.* San Francisco: Collins Publishers, 1993.

Csikszentimihalyi, M. and O. Beattie. "Life Themes: A Theoretical and Empirical Exploration of Their Origins and Effects." *Journal of Humanistic Psychology,* 19:1, pps. 45-63.

Custer, Gerald. *Provoking Meaning: Some Thoughts About Choral Hermeneutics. The Choral Journal,* November, 2001.

Covey, Stephen R. *The Seven Habits of Highly Effective People.* New York: Simon and Schuster, 1990.

Dawkins, Richard. *Unweaving The Rainbow.* New York: Houghton-Mifflin, 1998.

de Chardin, Teilhard. *The Phenomenon of Man.* New York: Harper and Row, 1959.

DeMello, Anthony. *Awareness: The Perils and Opportunities of Reality.* New York: Doubleday, 1990.

DeMello, Anthony. *Sadhana—A Way to God: Christian Exercises in Eastern Form.* New York: Doubleday, 1984.

Dillard, A. *The Writing Of Life.* San Francisco: HarperPerennial, 1989.

Dostoevsky, Fyodor. *The Brothers Karamazov.* Translated and annotated by Richard Pevear and Larissa Volokhonsky. New York: Vintage Books, 1991.

Dowrick, Stephanie. *Intimacy and Solitude.* New York: W.W. Norton, 1991.

Eckhart, Meister. *The Best of Meister Eckhart.* New York: Crossroads Publishing, 1998.

Feldschuh, Michael. The September 11 Photo Project. New York: HarperCollins, 2002.

Eckhart, Meister. *Meister Eckhart from Whom God Hid Nothing.* Boston: Shambala, 1996.

Feiss, Hugh. *Monastic Wisdom.* New York: Harper-Collins, 2000.

Fulghum, Robert. *All I Really Need to Know I Learned in Kindergarten.* New York: Ivy Books, 1988.

Fulghum, Robert. *Words I Wish I Wrote.* New York: Harper-Collins, 1997.

Gardiner, Howard. *Frames of Mind: The Theory of Multiple Intelligences.* San Francisco: Basic, 1990.

Gardner, Howard. "The Making of a Storyteller." *Psychology Today,* March, 1982, pps. 49-63.

Geertz, C. *Works and Lives: The Anthropologist as Author.* Stanford: Standford University Press, 1988.

Gomes, Peter. *The Good Life: Truths Last In Times of Need.* San Francisco: Harper, 2002.

Gomes, Peter. *Sermons: Biblical Wisdom for Daily Living.* New York: Avon Books, 1998.

Gyatso, Teazin. *Essence of the Heart Sutra.* Boston: Wisdom Publishing, 2002.

Harris, Frederick. *Conducting with Feeling.* Galesville, Maryland: Meredith Music Publications, 2001.

Heidigger, Martin. *Being and Time.* New York: Harper and Row, 1962.

Herford, Julius. "The Conductor's Search." *The Choral Journal 32,* December 1991: pps. 23–26.

Heschel, Abraham Joshua. *I Asked for Wonder.* New York: Crossroad Publishing, 1998.

Heschel, Abraham Joshua. *God in Search of Man.* New York: The Noon Day Press, 1955.

Heschel, Abraham Joshua. *Who is Man?* Stanford: Stanford University Press, 1965.

Hillman, James. *A Blue Fire.* New York: Harper and Row, 1989.

Hillman, James. *Kinds of Power: A Guide to its Intelligent Uses.* New York: Doubleday, 1995.

Hillman, James. *The Soul's Code: In Search of Character and Calling.* New York: Random House, 1996.

Hillman, James. *The Thought of the Heart and the Soul of the World.* Woodstock, CT, 1981.

Hillman, James. *Re-Visioning Psychology.* New York: Harper Perennial Publishers, 1992.

Holy Transfiguration Monastery, Trans. *The Ascetical Homilies of Saint Isaac the Syrian.* Boston: Holy Transfiguration Monastery, 1984.

Hopkins, Jeffrey. *Cultivating Compassion.* New York: Broadway Books, 2001.

John XXIII. *Journal of a Soul: The Autobiography of Pope John XXIII.* New York: Doubleday, 1964.

Joyce, James. *A Portrait of the Artist as a Young Man.* New York: Penguin, (1916) reprint, 1976.

Jordan, James. "The Case Study: The Nature, Description and Implications for Research Designs in Music Education." *Southeastern Journal of Music Education.* Volume 1, 1989, p. 51-60.

Kennedy, Caroline. *Profiles in Courage For Our Time.* New York: Hyperion, 2002.

Laudermilch, Kenneth. *An Understandable Approach To Musical Expression.* Galesville, Maryland: Meredith Music Publications, 2000.

Levitt, Jo Ann. *Sibling Revelry.* New York: Random House, 2001.

Levoy, Gregg. *Callings: Finding and Following an Authentic Life.* New York: Harmony Books, 1997.

Lesser, Elizabeth. *The New American Spirituality.* New York: Random House, 1999.

Lionni, Leo. *Frederick.* New York: Alfred A. Knopf, 1967.

Manning, Greg. *Love, Greg and Lauren.* New York: Bantam Books, 2002.

Marty, Martin and Micah Marty. *When True Simplicity is Gained: Finding Spiritual Clarity in a Complex World.* Grand Rapids, Michigan: William B. Eerdmans Publishing, 1998.

Masson, Jeffrey Moussaieff. *Dogs Never Lie About Love.* New York: Three Rivers Press, 1997.

McElroy, Susan Chernak. *Animals as Guides for the Soul.* New York: Ballantine, 1998.

Merton, Thomas. *A Search for Solitude.* San Francisco: Harper, 1997.

Meyer, Leonard B. *Emotion and Meaning in Music.* Chicago: University of Chicago Press, 1956.

Miller, Arthur I. *Einstein, Picasso: Space, Time, and the Beauty That Causes Havoc.* New York: Basic Books, 2001.

Miller, John. *Education and The Soul: Toward a Spiritual Curriculum.* Albany: State University of New York, 2000.

Mitchell, C and Weber, S. *Reinventing Ourselves As Teachers Beyond Nostalgia.* London: Falmer Press, 1999.

Moore, Thomas. *Original Self.* New York: Harper-Collins Publishers, 2000.

Naht Hahn, Thich. *Anger: Wisdom for Cooling the Flames.* New York: Riverhead Books, 2001.

Naht Hahn, Thich. *Call Me By My True Names: Collected Poems of Thich Naht Hahn.* Berkley: Parallax Press, 1999.

Naht Hahn, Thich. *Interbeing.* Berkeley: Parallax Press, 1998.

Naht Hahn, Thich. *Living Buddha, Living Christ.* New York: Riverhead Books, 1995.

Musician's Spirit

Naht Hahn, Thich. *Old Path, White Clouds.* California: Parallax, 1991.

Naht Hahn, Thich. *Miracle of Mindfulness.* Boston: Beacon Press, 1976.

Naht Hanh, Thich. *Peace Is Every Step: The Path of Mindfulness in Everyday Life.* New York: Bantam Books, 1991.

Naht Hahn, Thich. *Plum Village Chanting and Recitation Book.* Berkeley: Parallax Press, 2000.

Naht Hahn, Thich. *Present Moment, Wonderful Moment.: Mindfulness Verses For Daily Living.* Berkeley, California: Parallax Press, 1990.

Naht Hahn, Thich. *Teachings on Love.* Berkeley: Parallax Press, 1998.

Nash, Grace C. *That We Might Live.* Scottsdale, Arizona: Shano Publishers, 1984.

Newberg, Andrew, Eugene D'Aquili, and Vince Rause. *Why God Won't Go Away:* Brain Science and the Biology of Belief. New York: Ballantine Books, 2001.

Nietzsche, Friedrich. *Human, All Too Human.* Lincoln: University of Nebraska Press, 1984.

O'Donohue, John. *Anam Cara.* New York: Bantam Books, 1999.

O'Donohue, John. *Eternal Echoes: Exploring Our Hunger To Belong.* New York: Bantam Books, 1998.

O'Murchu, Diarmuid. *Quantum Theology.* New York: The Crossroad Publishing Company, 1997.

Palmer, Parker J. *The Courage to Teach: Exploring the Inner Landscape of a Teacher's Life.* San Francisco: Jossey-Bass Publishers, 1998.

Raines, Howell and Scott, Janny. *Portraits: 9/11/01. The Collected Portraits of Grief from The New York Times.* New York: Times Books, 2002.

Randall, William Lowell. *Biographical Aging and The Journey of Life.* Toronto: Praeger Press, 2000.

Randall, William Lowell. *The Stories We Are: An Essay of Self-Creation.* Toronto: University of Toronto Press, 1995.

Reeve, Christopher. *Still Me.* New York: Random House, 1998.

Richards, Mary Caroline. *Centering. Middleton,* Connecticut: Wesleyan University Press, 1989.

Richman, Sophia. *A Wolf in the Attic.* New York: Haworth Press, 2002.

Ricoeur, P. *Oneself As Another.* Chicago: The University of Chicago Press, 1992.

Rilke, Ranier Maria. *Letters to a Young Poet.* New York: W. W. Norton and Company, 1962.

Rinpoche, S. *The Tibetan Book of Living and Dying.* San Francisco: Harper, 1994.

Rowling, *J.K. Harry Potter and The Sorcerer's Stone.* New York: Scholastic, 1998.

Shaw, Robert. "Letters to a Symphony Chorus." *The Choral Journal.* 26, April 1986: pps. 5–8.

Shaw, Robert. *Preparing a Masterpiece: The Brahms Requiem.* Carnegie Hall. Videocassette.

Shields, Robert. *Cats, fish and Fools: The Lives and Art of Robert Shields.* Boston: Journey Editions, 1996.

Shoemaker, Fred. *Extraordinary Golf: The Art of the Possible.* New York: G. Putnam and Sons, 1996.

Stanislavski, Constantin. *An Actor Prepares.* New York: Routledge, 1964.

Stepanek. Mattie J.T. *Heartsongs.* New York: Hyperion, 2001.

Stepanek, Mattie J.T. *Hope Through Heartsongs.* New York: Hyperion, 2002.

St. Ruth, Diana. *Sitting.* New York: Penguin, 1998.

Stepanek, Mattie J.T. *Journey Through Heartsongs.* Alexandria, Virginia: VSP Books, 2001.

Swan, Howard. *Conscience of a Profession.* Chapel Hill, North Carolina: Hinshaw Music, Inc.

Thoreau, Henry David. *Walden,* 1854. Princeton: Princeton University Press, 1989.

Tillich, Paul. *The Courage To Be.* New Haven: Yale University Press, 1952.

Trungpa, Chögyam. *Cutting Through Spiritual Materialism.* Boston and London: Shambhala Publications, 1973.

Underhill, Evelyn. *Mysticism.* New York: Meridian Books, 1974.

Van Manen, M. *The Tact of Teaching: The Meaning of Pedagogical Thoughtfulness.* Albany: The State University of New York, 1991.

Vertosick, Frank T. *The Genius Within.* New York: Harcourt, 2002.

Walsch, Neale Donald. *Communion with God.* New York: G. Putnam's, 2000.

Walsch, Neale Donald. *Meditations from Conversations with God.* New York: Berkley Books, 1997.

Vonnegut, Kurt. *Breakfast of Champions.* New York: Bantam, 1973.

Weil, Simone. *Waiting For God.* New York: Harper and Row, 1951.

White, Perry D. *The Whole Conductor: Weston Noble's Philosophies on the Psychology of Conducting and Musicianship.* DMA Dissertation. Norman, Oklahoma: The University of Oklahoma, 1998.

Williams, James G. *The Girard Reader.* New York: The Crossroad Publishing Company, 1996.

Williamson, John Finley. "Choral Singing: [articles individually titled]." Twelve articles in Etude 68 and 69, April 1950–October 1951.

Williamson, John Finley. "The Conductor's Magic." *Etude* 69, April 1951: p. 23.

Williamson, John Finley. "Training the Individual Voice through Choral Singing." *Proceedings of the Music Teachers National Association* 33, 1938: pps. 52–59.

Zaleski, Philip. *The Best Spiritual Writing: 2000.* San Francisco: Harper, 2000.

Zukav, Gary. *The Seat of the Soul.* New York: Simon and Schuster, 1990.

recommended videos

Baraka: A World Beyond Words. Magdison Films, 1992.

Baraka, an ancient Sufi word with forms in many languages, translates as a blessing, or as a breath or essence of life from which the evolutionary process unfolds. A transcendently poetic tour of the globe, Baraka was shot in 24 countries on six continents.

Set to life affirming rhythms of various rituals, Baraka is a visualization of the interconnectedness humans share with the earth. Spanning such diverse locales as China, Brazil, Kuwait and major US and European cities, Baraka not only captures the harmony, but also the calamity that humans and nature have visited upon the earth. This film, perhaps more than any other, can serve to help artists connect with the world at large by taking them on a tour of the world that they do not know or have not experienced.

Morrie: Lessons on Living.
Buena Vista Home Entertainment/ABC News (19421-1)

This is the original set of interviews done by Ted Koppel for Nightline with Morre Schwartz, the subject of the book, Tuesdays with Morrie. All musicians should watch this video and take a life story journey with this great human being. His life lessons can travel far to help us in our music making.

Great Preachers: Peter Gomes
Odyssey Productions, LTD. www.gatewayfilms.com

In the age of rapidly developing media many have thought preaching was a dying craft from a bygone era. This video presents an actual sermon by Peter Gomes with an accompanying interview of Dr. Gomes.

Musician's Spirit

Yo-Yo Ma. Sarabande.
Bach Suite No.4 for Unaccompanied Cello. Film by Atom Egoyan and Niv Fichman. Sony Classical; DVD and Video.

A great musician instinctively builds a complex and intimate relationship with his listeners. Director Atom Egoyan's dramatic film explores a number of such relationships, revealing the generosity of spirit and love that flow from Yo-Yo Ma's performance of the Bach Fourth Suite.

Robert Shields: Celebration of Imagination.
Robert Shields Designs, Sedona, AZ.

The video, Robert Shields-Celebration of Imagination, is a rare montage of Robert Shields' performances with clips from his days in Union Square, the Shields & Yarnell Show, live appearances with the symphony, live work on stage, a peek at his life today and much more. The video makes a great companion for the hardcover book listed in the bibliography of this book. It is a documentary of a remarkable life story of an artist.

index of quoted persons

G

H

J

K

L

M

N

O

P

R

S

T

V

W

topic index

This index is designed for times when, before a rehearsal or performance, one is hunting for a piece of motivation or insight either to connect with oneself or with others.

about the author

One of America's most respected choral conductors and educators, James Jordan is associate professor of conducting at Westminster Choir College of Rider University, a leading center for the study and performance of choral music, where he is conductor of the Westminster Chapel Choir.

Dr. Jordan's unique educational background in conducting, the psychology of music, dance education, and psychology allow him to make poignant observations into the music-making process from the vantage point of a conductor.

An internationally recognized pedagogue, his theories of rhythm pedagogy and movement are now widely applied in music education for the teaching of rhythm to children and adults. His four textbooks and several videos on the subjects of Group Vocal Technique, Ensemble Diction, and Conducting are used for the education of teachers and conductors around the world. His conducting text, *Evoking Sound* was his first book with GIA Publications.

Prior to his appointment to the distinguished Westminster faculty, he served as chair for music education at the Hartt School of Music. He has also held positions at the School of the Hartford Ballet and the Pennsylvania State University. He holds degrees from Susquehanna University (BM) and Temple University (MM and Ph.D.). His study in the psychology of music has been with Edwin E. Gordon. His conducting teachers have been Elaine Brown, Wilhelm Ehmann, Volker Hempfling, and Gail B. Poch.

Website: evokingsound.com

about the visual artists

Michael Kinney

Michael Kinney started taking pictures with a Rollieflex that his grandfather gave him when he began high school. His acceptance into a five week program at the Pennsylvania Governor School for the Arts, studying under Terry Wild gave him real perspective to the possibilities of his medium. He attended the Rochester Institute of Technology, studying Fine Art Photography. Michael spent his Junior year at Salzburg College in Austria, he was deeply effected by what he saw of Europe's history in the Arts. Then returning to the states during a critical time he left school.

Michael eventually found himself living in a artist squatting community in NYC. After an eventful two years of life in the city, he left and traveled west to Seattle where he met Zen Master Chung Goh Sunim. Since 1989, Michael has been living and studying under his guidance. The work presented here is a blossom of this time. Pursuing his study of Zen Buddhist and Taoist practices, Michael Kinney currently resides at The Sixth Patriarch Zen Center in Berkeley, CA.

Daniel Payn

As a pilot of gliders and power aircraft as well as a drummer involved with classical music, jazz, punk, and emo bands, Daniel Payn is a high school senior who has had the opportunity to interact with very diverse groups of people. His early photographs were primarily abstract images of objects or nature in Vermont, where he spends his summers as a line crew chief at the Warren-Sugarbush airport. His photos have also been taken in the Sedona, Arizona area, where he has hiked extensively with family throughout his life.

Daniel's more recent work explores human interaction using a philosophical basis to provide social commentary. His work has been seen at exhibits in Vermont and Pennsylvania where he lives, and he plans to begin collegiate study next year in a program devoted to fine art photography and philosophy.

Daniel's image in this book was taken on the Mogollon Rim in Arizona, and was among the first of his award-winning works.

Yolanda Durán

Yolanda Durán has worked both as a graphic designer and art teacher for close to a decade. During this time, she has participated in numerous exhibits throughout the city of Chicago including exhibits at the Mexican Fine Arts Center Museum, Noyes Cultural Arts Center, and the Humbolt Park Stables Gallery. Miss Durán holds degrees from the University of Illinois at Chicago (BFA) and from the Art Institute of Chicago (MFA).